CHALLENGING THE TEACHING EXCELLENCE FRAMEWORK

Great Debates in Higher Education is a series of short, accessible books addressing key challenges to and issues in Higher Education, on a national and international level. These books are research informed but debate driven. They are intended to be relevant to a broad spectrum of researchers, students, and administrators in higher education, and are designed to help us unpick and assess the state of higher education systems, policies, and social and economic impacts.

Recently published in this series:

The Marketisation of English Higher Education: A Policy Analysis of a Risk-Based System
Colin McCaig

Access to Success and Social Mobility through Higher Education: A Curate's Egg?
Edited by Stuart Billingham

Evaluating Scholarship and Research Impact: History, Practices, and Policy Development
Jeffrey W. Alstete, Nicholas J. Beutell, and John P. Meyer

Sexual Violence on Campus: Power-Conscious Approaches to Awareness, Prevention, and Response
Chris Linder

Higher Education, Access and Funding: The UK in International Perspective
Edited by Sheila Riddell, Sarah Minty, Elisabet Weedon, and Susan Whittaker

British Universities in the Brexit Moment: Political, Economic and Cultural Implications
Mike Finn

CHALLENGING THE TEACHING EXCELLENCE FRAMEWORK

Diversity Deficits in Higher Education Evaluations

EDITED BY

KATE CARRUTHERS THOMAS
Birmingham City University, UK

AMANDA FRENCH
Birmingham City University, UK

United Kingdom – North America – Japan – India
Malaysia – China

Emerald Publishing Limited
Howard House, Wagon Lane, Bingley BD16 1WA, UK

First edition 2020

Reprints and permissions service
Contact: permissions@emeraldinsight.com

British Library Cataloguing in Publication Data
A catalogue record for this book is available from the British Library

ISBN: 978-1-78769-536-8 (Print)
ISBN: 978-1-78769-533-7 (Online)
ISBN: 978-1-78769-535-1 (Epub)

Printed and bound by CPI Group (UK) Ltd, Croydon, CR0 4YY

ISOQAR certified
Management System,
awarded to Emerald
for adherence to
Environmental
standard
ISO 14001:2004.

Certificate Number 1985
ISO 14001

INVESTOR IN PEOPLE

CONTENTS

PREFACE: TEACHING EXCELLENCE AS 'INSTITUTIONAL POLISHING'?

Kate Carruthers Thomas and Amanda French

INTRODUCTION

Taking as its starting point Barad's assertion that '*The optic/ apparatus for observations will determine what is seen*', this edited collection offers a lively and thought-provoking discussion about gendered, raced and classed implications of the Teaching Excellence Framework (TEF) in the United Kingdom's increasingly neoliberal higher education (HE) sector. The essays in this collection critically interrogate and cast doubt on the usefulness of the notion of 'excellence' to attempt to evaluate teaching in HE. In the process, they draw attention to the fact that mobilising unrealistic comparisons between higher education institutions (HEIs) around a reductionist conceptualisation of teaching excellence creates deficits through the inevitable difference that exists across institutions, disciplines and through the specific teaching interactions between individual lecturers and students in HE.

This introductory essay both outlines the content of the collection and invites readers to consider whether the performativity of 'excellence' in the TEF bears comparison to Ahmed's concept of 'institutional polishing': the labour of creating shiny surfaces (Ahmed, 2017, p. 102). Ahmed originally invokes the term 'institutional polishing' in relation to the performativity of diversity within HEIs (2012, 2017). This essay proposes that while explicitly stating a concern with teaching provision, learning gain and student outcomes for 'disadvantaged' students, the relationship between diversity and excellence in TEF rings hollow in relation to staff diversity, diversity in HE provision and different disciplinary and personal teaching styles. TEF and its associated matrixes and information therefore risk being a form of 'institutional speech act', that is, they collectively create corporate statements which do 'not go beyond pluralist understandings of diversity and are non-performative in the sense that they fail to deliver what they have promised' (2006, p.764). Furthermore, analyses predating the TEF of teaching excellence (Greatbatch & Holland, 2016), performativity (Ball, 2003) and quality assurance (Morley, 2001) highlight the complexity of the microprocesses and power structures involved in performing teaching excellence which the TEF signally fails to address or even acknowledge.

LET'S GET ETYMOLOGICAL

Excellence is a word with lofty origins from the Latin *excellentia* meaning superior; from *excellentum* meaning towering, distinguished; from *excellere*, meaning to surpass, be superior (Online Etymology Dictionary, 2020). Excellence is, therefore, relational in character. Yet in contemporary UK HE, excellence has become ubiquitous! Academics and institutional managers working in this competitive, marketised arena (Gourlay & Stevenson, 2017, p. 392) are continuously pressured to demonstrate excellence of teaching through the TEF; research through the Research Excellence Framework (REF) will shortly grapple with the KEF – the Knowledge Exchange Framework. Excellence is now a key source of reputational advantage and sector-wide comparisons within the increasingly neoliberal UK HE landscape. The ubiquity of excellence is, however, not surprising if we consider it in the context of performativity.

THE PERFORMATIVITY OF EXCELLENCE

Ball views performativity 'as one of three interrelated policy technologies of the UK education reform "package"' (2003, p. 216), the other two being the market and managerialism:

> *Performativity is a technology, a culture and a mode of regulation that employs judgements, comparisons and displays as means of incentive, control, attrition and change based on rewards and sanctions both material and symbolic.*

> (Ball, 2003)

Let's examine the ways in which the performativity of excellence mobilised in the TEF fulfils the three key functions in Ball's definition. Firstly, the TEF invites reward or sanction in a moment of promotion or inspection. The Government White Paper, *Success as a knowledge economy* (Department for Business, Innovation and Skills, 2016), legislated that from 2020, TEF awards would determine whether or not providers were permitted to raise tuition fees, thereby creating a link between the material 'quality' of an institution (symbolically

freighted as Gold, Silver or Bronze) and what they could
charge for their provision. Although recent and rapid changes
in UK government have delayed this ruling, governments'
intention to reward – or sanction – HEIs through the TEF
rankings remains. The status and market dynamics created by
the TEF are already in play. For example, they are clearly
signalled through marketing campaigns that proclaim an
institution's TEF Gold status at every opportunity. Even
though recent research by UCAS (2018) suggested students
and parents have very little idea what it actually means, it was
clear they viewed it very positively as a market proxy for
quality. Thus, the TEF process appears to have successfully
abstracted complex social, educational processes (though it's
various matrixes and contextual information) into potent
symbolic rankings. Increasingly, these rankings unproblematically facilitate comparison between institutions in
much the same ways as the REF tries to. Thirdly, in doing so,
the TEF requires every institution to 'fabricate a formal textual account' (Ball, 2003, p. 225) of its performance of
teaching excellence, which is submitted or 'displayed' in return
for a rating. This, however, clearly does not actually tell students much about the teaching they might actually experience
once they begin their studies.

Morley's pre-TEF perspective on quality assurance as 'a
process of reform or modernisation of public services …
which has created considerable pressure to produce and
perform' (2001, p. 465) echoes Ball's perspective on performativity in its claim that 'the results of audit provide a
reified reading, which becomes a truth… encoded in league
tables' (2001, p. 476). A reward/sanction binary is also visible
in her argument, 'for those at the top there is an artificial halo
effect for universities at the bottom of the league tables,
identity is a form of negative equity' (2001, p. 472). However,

Morley also pays attention to the effects of the quality assurance process at the micro level, arguing that any damage to institutional reputation as a result of a blanket quality assurance judgement becomes an attack on the competence of every organisational member. Regarding the TEF, it is striking that it is often HE lecturers, delivering the teaching, who are least likely to be involved in TEF processes. Furthermore, Morley identifies the way a one-size-fits-all quality assurance like the TEF creates its own structures and systems of power and exposes the micropolitics of gendered/racialised/able-bodied and classed power in organisations. Again this, as we discuss in this collection, affects those HE lecturers who are interacting with students and delivering teaching on a daily basis and who become most subject to TEF-related processes and judgements.

TEACHING EXCELLENCE AND DIVERSITY DEFICITS (BOOK TITLE)

The seven essays in this collection address varying aspects of power and micropolitics embedded in TEF and notions of teaching excellence. In 'Elusive and elastic, and 'incorrigibly plural': definitions and conceptualisations of teaching excellence', Saunders, Moore and Zimbars offer a critical consideration of the notion of 'excellence' underpinning the performative measures of TEF in a neoliberal, marketised sector. In their companion piece, Operationalising teaching excellence in higher education: from 'sheep-dipping' to 'virtuous practice', the same authors take a critical look at mechanisms for developing teaching excellence, specifically, developing capability and rewarding success and pedagogy. Their approach problematises the entanglement of individual academics' teaching identities with their employers' commercial goals and market position and questions the validity and reliability of how TEF measures 'excellent teaching', specifically in relation to those academic staff least powerfully positioned in the system. The pernicious effects of such micropolitics, especially when they go unacknowledged, are explored in Bartram's queer analysis of the TEF in Chapter 6 *Queering the TEF*, while in Chapter 3, Crockford's analysis, '*Wishing Won't Make It So....': Strategic ambiguity, Policy Ad hoc'ery, Deliverology and the Wickidity of TEF's Equality and Diversity Aspirations*, critiques 'the requirement to fabricate a formal textual account' (Ball, 2003, p. 225) of teaching excellence in return for a rating.

The TEF highlights an explicit concern with teaching provision, learning gain and student for 'disadvantaged' students (ref). Yet in Chapter 4, *Rapport and Relationships: The Student Perspective on Teaching Excellence*, Lawrence, Hunt, Shaw and Symonie offer a number of firsthand accounts of how students from a widening participating background actually perceive quality teaching. These accounts are far removed from National Student Survey data, currently the main evaluation survey used in TEF metrics. Moreover, diversity in HE is not confined to students; HE staff are of all genders, of diverse class, ethnic and national background, age, faith and sexual orientation. Yet, student evaluation surveys used by TEF as measures of excellence are biased against female and minority ethnic staff already overrepresented in lower grades and more precarious roles within the sector. This is the issue discussed by French in Chapter 5, '*It's not what gets taught, or how well it may be taught, but who is doing the teaching': Can student evaluations ever deliver a fair assessment on teaching excellence in* HE? French makes clear how academic career progression is entwined with the TEF (and

REF) yet argues that racial and sexual prejudices (amongst others) and stereotyping make it more difficult for some staff to 'perform' excellence. Equally, structural conditions of precarity and minority exacerbate the employment and career impacts of not doing so.

Working in HE is the only option available for academics who are passionate about teaching their subjects and their students. Must they then, to an extent, become complicit with the daily enactment of excellence in a sector shaped by the ideology of neoliberalism? In Chapter 7, Brogan's essay, *Diversity Deficits: Resisting the TEF*, explores how lecturers might push back against such complicity working with their students to create alternative, potentially disruptive spaces for teaching and learning. If, as Ahmed argues, institutional polishing is the labour of creating shiny surfaces resulting in the fabrication of a 'textual account' of diversity through which an organisation can reflect back a good image to itself, we must 'be careful not to lose ourselves in the reflection' (Ahmed, 2017, p. 102).

TEACHING EXCELLENCE AS 'INSTITUTIONAL POLISHING'?

In closing, let's return to the question: does the performativity of 'excellence' in the TEF bear comparison to Ahmed's concept of 'institutional polishing'? Ahmed argues that when the labour of polishing is successful, the image is shiny. 'The labor removes the very traces of labor …' (Ahmed, 2017, p. 102). Institutional polishing is therefore closely allied to her definition of an 'institutional speech act' whereby

> …*a diversity policy can come into existence without coming into use … such policies can be 'institutional*

> speech acts' which do not go beyond pluralist
> understandings of diversity and non-performative in
> the sense that they fail to deliver what they have
> promised.

(2006, p. 764).

Applying this argument to teaching (and/or research) excellence, institutional polishing results in the fabrication of a 'textual account' of excellence (Ball, 2003, p. 225) and the 'reified reading which becomes a truth' (Morley, 2001, p. 476). In this way, the TEF facilitates institutional polishing by creating an institutional speech act of 'teaching excellence' which is largely performative and restricted to the narrow criteria established by TEF metrics. This results in a failure to address the actual complexity of the relationship between teaching excellence and diversity in HE.

Neither is it enough to understand how shiny surfaces create convincing reflections. We must also appreciate what is obscured. As Ahmed warns, 'When something is shiny, so much is not reflected' (2006, p. 764). This brings us to a second question: what is *not* shown in the performance of teaching excellence? As previously noted, 'performing' teaching excellence does not mean we need to remain ignorant of the ideology at its root, nor of the relationships of power which keep it in play, nor of the complex social processes of teaching and learning which TEF claims its metrics distil (but which we argue they cannot). The inherent structural inequalities of society, which are tacitly replicated within the academy, universities and the HE sector as a whole, are also visible in the TEF – disadvantaging women and people of colour, people with disabilities and different sexual orientations. Indeed, the reflected glory of TEF's misleading coda of 'excellence' obscures a glaring dissonance between the artificial performativity of teaching excellence and actual lived experiences of diversity.

REFERENCES

Ahmed, S. (2006). *Queer phenomenology: Orientations, objects, others*. Durham, NC: Duke University Press.

Ahmed, S. (2012). *On being included: Racism and diversity in institutional life*. Durham, NC: Duke University Press.

Ahmed, S. (2017). *Living a feminist life*. Durham, NC: Duke University Press.

Ball, S. J. (2003). The teacher's soul and the terrors of performativity. *Journal of Education Policy*, *18*(2), 215–228.

Department for Business, Innovation and Skills. (2016). Success as a knowledge economy: Teaching excellence, social mobility and student choice. London: The Stationary Office (CM9258).

Gourlay, L., & Stevenson, J. (2017). Teaching excellence in higher education: Critical perspectives. *Teaching in Higher Education*, *22*(4), 391–395.

Greatbatch, D., & Holland, J. (2016). *Teaching quality in higher education: Literature review and qualitative research*. London: BIS.

Morley, L. (2001). Subjected to review: Engendering quality and power in higher education. *Journal of Education Policy*, *16*(5), 465–478.

Online Etymology Dictionary (2020). *excellence [online]*. Retrieved from https://etymonline.com/word/excellence. Accessed on June 22, 2020.

UCAS (2018). *UCAS analysis shows growing awareness of the TEF among applicants to higher education [online]*. Retrieved from https://www.ucas.com/corporate/news-and-key-documents/news/ucas-analysis-shows-growing-awareness-tef-among-applicants-higher-education. Accessed on June 22, 2020.

.

1

ELUSIVE AND ELASTIC, AND 'INCORRIGIBLY PLURAL': DEFINITIONS AND CONCEPTUALISATIONS OF TEACHING EXCELLENCE

John Sanders, Joanne Moore, and Anna Mountford-Zimdars

ABSTRACT

This chapter provides an introduction to the problematic notion of teaching excellence in higher education, which is a focus of this collection. It draws on an extensive review of relevant literature to explore how teaching excellence is defined and conceptualised and what factors underpin different conceptions. It notes that definitions are disparate, often context-specific and are influenced by a range of different 'players'. It then examines how different conceptualisations play out at the macro, meso and micro levels and highlights the tensions between performative and transformative notions of teaching excellence. It notes the move from 'surface' to 'deep' excellence and efforts to articulate a more holistic conception of teaching excellence that emphasises the relational, emotional and moral dimensions of teaching. It suggests that, rather than seeking singular definitions and conceptions, it may be more useful to talk of 'teaching excellences', to reflect a stratified and plural sector, a diverse student body and different disciplinary families. Equally, it argues for further investigation of the intersections of teaching excellence with other key drivers of institutional change, such as student engagement and well-being, inclusion and diversity, widening participation and retention and success.

Keywords: Teaching excellence; higher education; teaching quality; learning and teaching; teaching excellence framework; institutional change

INTRODUCTION

Twenty years on from the Dearing Report's prescription for 'national excellence in teaching and the management of learning' in higher education, to be achieved within two decades (NCIHE, 1997), the fledgling Teaching Excellence Framework (TEF) finally emerged in the 2017 Higher Education and Research Act as a controversial new feature of the HE landscape. Floated in a Green Paper (BIS, 2015) and fleshed out in the subsequent White Paper and technical consultation documents (BIS, 2016a; 2016b), the TEF aimed to 'drive up the standard of teaching in all universities' (2016a, p. 13) and to inform student choice, as well as potentially allowing up to 80% of providers to increase their tuition fees (QAA, 2015). This link between meeting teaching excellence criteria and the ability to charge higher tuition fees, alongside the reputational implications of the quasi-Olympian categorisation of institutions, has ensured that the excellence in teaching agenda has moved to a pivotal position in the priorities of universities.

The Higher Education Green Paper *Teaching Excellence, Social Mobility and Student Choice* starts from the assumption that 'teaching is the poor cousin to research' (BIS, 2015, p. 8). In part, the TEF process reflects a desire to address the perceived imbalance between the research and teaching functions of universities (Blackmore, Blackwell, & Edmondson, 2016; Cashmore, Cane, & Cane, 2013; Locke, 2014) and to challenge the 'dominant rhetoric of excellence in research' (Gunn & Fisk, 2013, p. 10). As Skelton (2009) notes, citing Barnett (2003), 'teaching and research have become "rival ideologies" in the University, often competing for resources and personnel' (p. 110). The rebalancing of higher education's knowledge economy aims to 'build a culture where teaching has equal status with research' (Johnson, 2015), thereby returning to some extent to the historic, pre-Humboldtian teaching-centred origins of universities. This renewed focus on the status and importance of teaching, for all the contingent ideological differences and operational difficulties explored below, has been welcomed by commentators and HE lecturers alike (Bartram, Hathaway, & Rao, 2019; Hubble, Foster, & Bolton, 2016; McGhee, 2016; Wood & Su, 2017).

However, for O'Leary and Wood (2018), the inauguration of the TEF represents a worrying 'turning point for the sector' (p. 4), whilst Brabon (2016) has characterised it as a Rubicon-crossing moment. As French (2017) points out, though, 'political interest in the quality of teaching standards' has a long history in compulsory education and has been signalled consistently in government publications on higher education since the time of the Dearing Report (p. 5). The long march to this pivotal point began some time ago. Indeed, as Little, Locke, Parker, and Richardson (2007) note: 'Since the late 1990s, more explicit attention has been given to higher education teaching and learning through the development of institutional teaching and learning strategies, linked to broader underlying mission statements' (p. 1). There have also been several policy-driven initiatives across some or all the four UK nations, including Teaching Quality Assessments and Subject Reviews (until 2001), the National Teaching Fellowship Scheme (NTFS: 2000 onwards), Centres of Excellence in Teaching and Learning (CETLs: 2005–2010) and the UK Professional Standards Framework (UKPSF: 2003 onwards). All have placed an increasing emphasis on the importance of university teaching and its professionalisation. The role of the Higher Education Academy (HEA), created in 2003, has been central to a number of these initiatives and to the articulation of notions of teaching excellence.

The emphasis on teaching excellence mirrors a sharper policy focus on student engagement and 'the student experience', both vigorously contested concepts (see, Taylor & Robinson, 2012 and Sabri, 2011). It also reflects the increasing importance attached to student-orientated learning and teaching (Trigwell, 2010; 2012) and to the outcomes of a university education. In an increasingly differentiated and marketised sector (John & Fanghanel, 2015) operating during a period of economic turbulence, notions of value for money, rhetoric about student choice (Brown & Carasso, 2013) and debates about the purposes of universities and the relative importance of the different roles of universities (see Barnett, 2010) have increasingly come to the fore. In addition, some commentators argue that technology, eLearning and the mass scale of higher education have fundamentally changed teaching and the nature of interactions with students (De Courcy, 2015).

The strong reemergence of a discourse around excellence in teaching has been a worldwide phenomenon rather than just a UK-specific development (see, Brockerhoff, Strensaker & Huisman, 2014; Brusoni et al., 2014; De Courcy, 2015; Henard & Roseveare, 2012; Gunn & Fisk, 2013; Skelton, 2007); though, as Courtney (2016) predicted, the development of the TEF has placed England (and Northern Ireland) very much in the vanguard. Plenty of institutions, countries and transnational organisations have been talking about excellence in teaching, but few have put in place coherent national frameworks (Klemeric & Ashwin, 2015). As Nick Hillman of the Higher Education Policy Institute commented in 2016, there was 'no off-the-shelf solution available from another country' (HEPI, 2016).

Moreover, as Stephanie Marshall notes in her foreword to Gunn and Fisk's (2013) review, 'in the UK, and across the globe, there is little narrative around what is meant by "teaching excellence" and no country has defined an agreed concept of excellence in teaching' (p. 5). Whilst descriptors for research excellence are usually uniform, descriptors of teaching excellence vary greatly across and within institutions (Wespel, Orr, & Jaegar, 2013). Gunn and Fisk (2013) argue that there is 'a lack of sophistication in conceptualisation of university teaching excellence both generally but more particularly in terms of changing expectations and roles' (p. 7).

This chapter provides a broad overview of the research literature pertaining to teaching excellence and explores key definitions and conceptions of teaching excellence. It encompasses both published academic outputs (peer-reviewed articles and evaluative studies, earlier literature reviews and books) and key policy and governmental reports and a range of 'grey' literature (including unpublished institutional research, blogs, thought pieces and reviews) which pertain to teaching excellence. Much of this latter material has been the result of the publication of the Green and White Papers and, prior to that, of the successful divining of the direction of policy travel. The main focus is on material published in the last decade. However, the review cites earlier studies whose focus or findings remain current and relevant. Similarly, whilst the prime geographical concentration is on UK higher

education, international evidence is drawn on where particular insights or comparisons are judged to link directly to the
issues explored in this overview.

DEFINING AND CONCEPTUALISING TEACHING EXCELLENCE

Ground Clearing

A key challenge in conceptualising teaching excellence is that
this is 'a contested concept' (Macfarlane, 2007, p. 48), and a
compound one at that. It is 'socially constructed' (Rostan &
Vaira, 2011) and a 'notion that is riven with uncertainties that
reflect different political, social and intellectual positions'
(Knight, 2006, p. 637). As Bartram et al. (2019) note, the UK
government's case for introducing the TEF has been framed
explicitly in terms of notions of value for money, consumer
choice and free market ideology, working on the basis that

> *Competition between providers in any market
> incentivises them to raise their game, offering greater
> choice of more innovative and better quality
> products and services at lower cost. Higher
> Education is no exception.*

(BIS, 2016a, p. 8)

Critics of this approach, by contrast, 'reject the underlying
authoritarian assumptions about competition and performativity inherent in neoliberal ideology' in favour of 'a more
expansive view…which sees academic practices of teaching,
scholarly activity and research as inter-connected' (Wood &
Su, 2017, p. 452). In this view, not only is 'teaching excellence' contested but so is the focus on teaching rather than
learning, as is the use of the term 'excellence' on its own.

Before exploring different dimensions of the notion of 'teaching excellence', it is worth noting the (perhaps obvious) point that 'teaching excellence' is not necessarily the same thing as 'teacher excellence' or 'excellent teaching', though there are many potential areas of overlap. Little et al. (2007), for example, note that 'excellent teaching' is often used in the context of microinteractions between teachers and students and in some research and policy documents is taken to be synonymous with 'effective teaching' (p. 2). Gunn and Fisk (2013) similarly see 'teacher excellence' as being related to individual philosophies and practices, whilst 'teaching excellence' pertains to overall system-wide conceptions of excellence (p. 19). For them 'teaching excellence embraces but is not confined to teacher excellence' (p. 7).

Equally, though it is widely recognised that the teacher delivering a course or module is a key factor in determining student outcomes (Gibbs, 2010), 'teaching excellence' and 'excellent student learning' are not the same thing, merely seen from a different angle. As Little et al. (2007) note, 'teaching and student learning are distinct, although related, phenomena' (p. 4) and 'excellence in student learning may or may not require excellent teaching' (p. 2). Gunn and Fisk's (2013) follow-up survey reiterates 'the difficulties of evaluating how excellence in teaching actually affects student learning'. Citing the different positions of Trigwell (2010) and Haggis (2004), they comment that 'quantitative measurements showing the cause and effect of teaching excellence on student learning have yet to be robustly articulated in the research literature' (p. 9). Strang, Bélanger, Manville and Meads (2016) and Lodge and Bonsanquet (2014) similarly note the limited range and 'grossly inadequate' nature of the empirical evidence underpinning measures of quality learning outcomes.

The developments of comparable measures in relation to teaching effectiveness in the schools sector (see, Kane,

McCaffrey, Miller, & Staiger, 2013) may be instructive, but
are rarely mentioned in the literature. In general, the HE
sector's challenges in terms of definition, delivery and measurement are not helped by its 'inability...to come to
some regularised consensus about what constitutes teaching
excellence, teacher excellence, excellent teaching as well as
excellent student learning' (Gunn & Fisk, 2013, p. 9). This
definitional impasse is noted in a number of recent surveys
(Brusoni et al., 2014; Greatbatch & Holland, 2016; Land &
Gordon, 2015; Strang et al., 2016), though at the level of
individual classroom practice, Bartram et al. (2019) report 'a
broadly shared definition of teaching excellence' amongst
academics (p. 5).

The term 'excellence' itself is not without its problems
(Glasner, 2003). These can be exacerbated by politicians'
often casual and profligate use of the word (Brusoni et al.,
2014) and by the different ways that it can be interpreted.
Greatbatch and Holland (2016), for example, outline the
differences between norm-referenced or criterion-referenced
conceptions of 'excellence'. Others question the current
value and meaning of the term. Stevenson, Burke, Whelan,
Sealey and Ploner's (2014) survey of over 350 'frontline'
teaching staff found many who 'reject outright the concept of
"excellence", which they frequently describe as a term that
has been co-opted and evacuated of pedagogical meaning' (p.
5). These views are echoed in the findings from Wood and Su's
(2017) small-scale survey and Bartram et al.'s (2019)
comparative study of the perspectives of English and Australian academics on the subject.

Historically, as Little et al. (2007) note, 'excellence' has
drifted in and out of the lexicon used to describe different
aspects of the quality of higher education provision. Its
meaning in relation to teaching has also shifted at times along
a continuum ranging from 'good enough' to 'actually very

good' to 'truly outstanding'. Equally, descriptors like 'effective', 'high quality' and 'excellent' are often used interchangeably. Strang et al.'s (2016) literature review for the HEA examines 'quality teaching', with 'quality' used as a noun adjunct. In the schools and FE sectors, comparable and equally slippery terms like 'outstanding' (derived from Ofsted's four-level rating system) and 'great teaching' (the subject of Coe, Aloisi, Higgins & Major's 2014 research review) hold sway.

'Good teaching' is the preferred term in Ashwin, Abbas and McLean's (2012) discussion of ways of defining, improving and measuring the quality of sociology-related undergraduate course. Similarly, Abbas, Brennan, Abbas, Gantogtokh and Bryman's (2016) study of 'teaching excellence in the disciplines' in the main talks about 'good teaching'. This cautious approach perhaps reflects the difficulties that Gunn and Fisk (2013) identify in articulating the differences between threshold quality and teaching excellence. In contrast, this study follows Little et al. (2007) and Brusoni et al. (2014) in believing that 'to excel', and therefore 'excellence', implies preeminence and possessing features that 'stand out from the rest' (p. 1). However, this raises some tricky questions when it comes to universalising teaching excellence. As Gunn and Fisk (2013) ask, 'what use will 'excellence' be as rhetorical device within university mission statements when we have all become excellent?' (p. 22).

~ary challenges were anticipated by writers) when he argued that excellence may be a hat the emphasis should be on raising the l rather than encouraging a few spikes of ving that 'it is easier to be a beacon on a dark urged that the sector's focus should be on standards across the board rather than indi- is approach was at the heart of Scotland's preference for continuous quality enhancement – in the form of Enhancement-led Institutional Reviews – rather than the establishment of CETLs in 2005. Wales similarly opted to focus on thematic and subject enhancement (Little et al., 2007, pp. 32–33). These tensions around the concept of excellence are sometimes reflected in the balancing acts of quality agencies reluctant to cite best practice exemplars for fear of setting the bar too high whilst simultaneously wishing to avoid normalising the attainment of threshold standards.

Teaching Excellence

'Teaching excellence', then, is not a value-free concept. Some researchers (for example, O'Leary & Wood, 2018; Shephard, Harland, Stein, & Tidswell, 2011) see it as part of a 'neoliberal, inherently "performative" agenda' (Gunn & Fisk, 2013, p. 47) and symptomatic of a move to a consumerist model of HE: a view shared by many HE lecturers (Bartram et al., 2019; Stevenson et al., 2014; Wood & Su, 2017). For Layton and Brown (2011), concepts of excellence are problematic and trivialise excellent teaching, whilst Clegg (2007) has argued that the concept should be abandoned in favour of 'good enough' teaching and support of learning. This conclusion is echoed in a critique of Ofsted's criteria for 'outstanding' teaching which argues that 'the current obsession with obtaining an "outstanding" judgement...threatens to undermine what is reasonable and possible in the pursuit of an unattainable perfection that in too many cases demoralises rather than motivates' (Richards, 2015, p. 237). In higher education, critics contend that excellence has become an 'empty and meaningless' concept (Wood & Su, 2017, p. 463), part of universities' market positioning and stock-in-trade boosterism, not worth the mission statement that it's written into (see Skelton, 2009, p. 107, referring to a motion carried at the 2007 HEA annual conference), a prescient view that has largely been confirmed by TEF's implementation.

A number of these themes are taken up in Stevenson et al.'s (2014) study of 'pedagogical stratification' which reveals a complex picture of 'institutions both striving to distinguish themselves as distinct while, at times, homogenising their approaches to teaching excellence, pedagogic practices and the overall student experience' (p. 5). This scenario is echoed in a commentary on an analysis of TEF2 provider submissions (Moore et al., 2017) in which HEA identifies the risk that 'as institutions seek to achieve Gold awards, teaching excellence becomes narrowed to a dominant interpretation of the TEF criteria and so leads to a homogenising of the sector, rather than a celebration of diversity' (HEA, 2017).

Stevenson et al.'s (2014) research also highlights tensions between a top-down performative approach which regards teaching excellence as something that can 'be quantified, codified and thus rewarded' and bottom-up student-focussed teaching practices 'enabling individual students, through critical pedagogies, to achieve their potential' (p. 5). Performative modes of assessing teaching excellence in this way follow market-orientated imperatives and frameworks, suppressing diversity and innovation of pedagogic approaches so that 'teaching... becomes technicist and performative rather than critical and transformative' (p. 5; see also, Burke, Stevenson, & Whelan, 2015).

This analysis is echoed in Ashwin's (2016a) characterisation of the dilemma that HE practitioners face in addressing the tension between 'the legitimacy of the call for good teaching' with 'the distorting tendency of "excellence"' and meeting 'the challenge of challenging teaching excellence'. This tension is similarly reflected in the concerns of Wood and Su's (2017) respondents that 'a genuine commitment to excellence in teaching may be reduced potentially to an evidence-gathering quality assurance process' (p. 460) and in the 'vast majority' of Bartram et al.'s (2019) English and Australian academics' belief in 'the positive educational dimensions of the concept' whilst voicing 'equally strong concerns about what they saw as the political/managerialist (ab)use of the term' (pp. 11–12). These fears are borne out in a comprehensive survey of UK lecturers commissioned by the University and College Union, which found that the TEF was 'having a greater impact on institutional policies of teaching and learning than the actual teaching of academic staff' (O'Leary, Cui, & French, 2019, p. 5).

Other commentators, whilst noting these cautions and accepting the difficulties and limitations of the concept of teaching excellence, posit a more pragmatic and positive response to its recent eminence. Gunn and Fisk (2013), for example, see it as an opportunity for 'developing a shared repertoire around teaching and teacher excellence which fulfils the requirements of the range of internal and external groups invested in facilitating excellent learning outcomes' (p. 48). Skelton (2009), one of the most prolific and considered writers on the subject, supports Nixon (2007) in reimagining teaching excellence as a moral category, whereby 'it is not sufficient to think of what "works" in our teaching and support of learning, but rather what is "good" – what is morally defensible and contributes to good in the world' (p. 110). In these terms, 'teaching excellence' can be distinguished from 'everyday' teaching in higher education' and can be viewed as the result of 'a serious commitment to the reflexive development of a value-laden and morally defensible practice' (p. 109).

As well as being contested, the research literature also acknowledges that definitions of 'teaching excellence' are disparate and often context dependent. The lack of consensus on how excellence is defined, operationalised and measured in relation to teaching and learning noted by Little at al. in 2007 remained true six years later in Gunn and Fisk's (2013) review. Their report provides an extensive and diverse list of 'different players in teaching excellence' (p. 9) and also notes how the educational goals, values and norms of government, employers, the academy and different disciplines may impact variably on how teaching excellence is defined and viewed in an institution (p. 12). In some cases, these drivers may be overlaid with the influence of professional bodies and external accreditation. In the new era of student engagement and students as partners (Healey, Flint & Harrigan, 2014; Trowler, 2010), student perceptions and perspectives (including those of alumni) have also come increasingly to the fore (Hammer et al., 2010; Su & Wood, 2012).

CONCEPTUALISATIONS OF TEACHING EXCELLENCE AT DIFFERENT LEVELS

How the interests of different stakeholders play out is illustrated by looking at the different levels of engagement with conceptions of teaching excellence. The macro level incorporates broad social and economic influences and sectoral and national government policies; the meso level takes in individual institutions, disciplines and departments; whilst the micro level focuses on individual courses, teacher–learner interactions and peer-to-peer learning. It is important to stress, however, that these are merely useful descriptors rather than being strict demarcation lines. For example, initiatives such as the CETLs, though conceived as a macro policy instrument and implemented at institution and departmental level, were in practice animated at the level of course team and individual enthusiasms.

At the macro level, teaching excellence has been historically equated with achievement of 'international standards' and aspirations to be 'world-class', with a view to competing globally not just in terms of the sector's status and recruitment potential but also in relation to national economic aims (Department for Education and Skills [DfES], 2003, NCIHE, 1997; Skelton, 2005). It has also been seen as a lever to facilitate greater efficiency and 'maximise individual, institutional and system performance' (Skelton, 2005, p. 30). Performative conceptions of teaching excellence thus emphasise measurement and control. In a macro context, these are often used implicitly, rather than always explicitly, but they remain powerful and persuasive, part of the taken for granted neoliberal 'new common sense' (Torres, 2013, cited in, Stevenson et al., 2014, p. 8; see also, O'Leary & Wood, 2018).

At the meso level, excellence is articulated in learning and teaching strategies and promoted in policies and practices (for example, in relation to recognition and reward). Stevenson et al. (2014) cite one institutional teaching and learning strategy in which 'the operational plan for staff was almost entirely comprised of awards-based recognition' (p. 17). Gunn and Fisk (2013) note that while it is 'essentially a contingent concept, necessarily assessed from "within", there is very little to distinguish teaching excellence in teaching-oriented and research-oriented institutions' (p. 7). The resulting conceptions, articulated in diverse universities, often mix aspirational language with pragmatic aims and purposes and are sometimes perceived as a tool to standardise and homogenise (Skelton, 2005), emphasising systems and quality processes over the content of teaching.

Many critics have highlighted this trend. Writing in 2003, Morley argued that 'the "culture of excellence" (quality, audit, performance indicators, managerialism, professionalisation, consumerism etc) has resulted in mediocrity' (p. 130, cited in

Little et al., 2007, p. 16). Barkas, Scott, Poppitt and Smith (2019) and O'Leary and Wood (2018) come to similar conclusions 15 years later. Other work on teaching 'excellence' and pedagogic stratification by Burke et al. (2015) has highlighted the significant gap between simply reciting and actually grasping the meanings behind key words and phrases from the lexicon of teaching excellence used by senior academics.

The meso level is at the heart of what Gunn and Fisk (2013) identified as one of the two dominant discourses related to teaching excellence – the belief that 'concepts of excellence currently being generated and manifested within organisational structures in universities are primarily part of a culture of performance management and measurement' (p. 14). This is a theme that surfaces in Abbas et al.'s (2016) interviews with deans in the social science cluster, particularly in relation to tensions between top-down centrally imposed (and often ill-defined) conceptions of teaching quality and discipline-based conceptions. It is also at the heart of a number of recent critiques of the TEF (Barkas et al., 2019; O'Leary & Wood, 2018; Wood & Su, 2017).

Yet the meso level is also the locus of some of the significant strides that have been made in the recognition and reward of teaching and the development of excellent practices – the other key discourse that Gunn and Fisk (2013) highlight. Wide-ranging debate, diverse approaches and experimentation about what teaching excellence means is revealed in the extensive practice-based literature and in the TEF2 provider submissions (Moore et al., 2017). However, there are few accounts that examine change driven by more than just performance-related diktats or individual enthusiasms or that rigorously evaluate integrated institutional or departmental initiatives. This gap means that system-wide, meso level conceptions of 'teaching excellence' (see, Gunn & Fisk, 2013, p. 19) are not fully accounted for in the literature.

At the micro level of individual course, teacher–learner interactions and peer-to-peer learning, teaching excellence is seemingly easier to identify. It is normally focused on individual performance and what Skelton (2005) terms the 'psychologised understandings of teaching excellence' (p. 24). This draws on

> ...humanistic, cognitive and, to a lesser extent behavioural psychology...[and]...is associated with the establishment of universal procedures for teaching and learning, their successful implementation in practice and the achievement of specified outcomes.

(p. 31)

This approach emphasises the extent to which teachers are student-focused and aim to bring about conceptual changes and intellectual development in their students. It is at this level that the theme of the recognition and reward of teaching (focussing on the importance of individual performance, informed by excellent practices, parity of esteem with research and dynamic engagement with students) – the second of the two dominant discourse identified by Gunn and Fisk (2013, p. 14) – primarily plays out. This discussion is represented graphically in Table 1.1.

In summarising the literature on different conceptions, Gunn and Fisk (2013) argue for an approach that recognises differences and tensions and

> ...a conceptualisation that avoids standardising teaching excellence into one harmonious category. Rather a process is needed that brings abstract

> *theorising from one or two parts of the academy*
> *(education and educational development), policy,*
> *and disciplinary practice together.*

(p. 20)

They also highlight the need to embrace both objective methods, techniques and interventions related to teaching excellence and the subjective and qualitative elements of teaching. Brockerhoff et al. (2014), writing about the Competition for Teaching Excellence in Germany, make a similar distinction between a 'structural' and a 'cultural' approach to teaching excellence. The former 'refers to direct and functional changes in the organisation of teaching and learning', while the latter approach 'is more indirect, emphasising the collective responsibility of academic staff in providing high-quality education' (p. 238). For Gunn and Fisk (2013), objective approaches often seek to identify a set of core competencies or behaviours that that can potentially be replicated and measured (Gibbs, 2007; Zhu, Wang, Cai, & Engels, 2013). However, they also raise concerns that 'teaching is being reduced to the acquisition of a set of competencies' (Fitzmaurice, 2010, p. 1) or a purely 'technicist' exercise (Stevenson et al., 2014), underpinned by a 'deliverology' discourse which privileges the student as consumer (Su & Wood, 2012, drawing on, Pring et al., 2009).

In contrast, for Dinetke, Dolmans, Wolfhangel and Van Der Vleuten (2004) and Skelton (2005), excellent teaching abilities extend beyond an easily describable set of skills, whilst Fitzmaurice (2010) emphasises the 'relational' aspect of teaching. This features prominently in Lubicz-Nawrocka and Bunting's (2019) analysis of student nominations for a teacher award scheme: these focussed on 'teachers' efforts, their commitment to engaging students, how they break

Table 1.1. Macro, Meso and Micro level Considerations for Teaching Excellence.

Level	Description	Teaching Excellence
Macro	Social and economic influences, sectoral and government policy	Excellence by international standards and aspirations to be 'world-class', excellence related to national economic aims and global competition.
Meso	Individual institutions/disciplines/departments	Institutional learning and teaching strategies and policies and practices. Teaching excellence initiatives, recognition, rewards and awards schemes. Tensions between central/discipline and top-down/bottom-up approaches.
Micro	Individual course and teacher–learner interactions, peer learning	Implementation of transformative, student-focused practices that link to individual teaching philosophies. Individual recognition and reward.

Source: Created by authors.

down student-teacher barriers, and how they provide stable support for students' (p. 14). Bartram et al.'s (2019) data (from academics) 'repeatedly highlighted the profoundly relational and dialogic dimension of TE, reliant on empathy, creativity, openness, enthusiasm and communicative engagement' (p. 9). As Burke and Crozier (2012) note, 'teaching is necessarily fraught with emotional as well as rational processes' (p. 6).

These more subjective and holistic conceptions of teaching are perhaps most fully and eloquently articulated in Skelton's (2009) vision that teaching excellence

- involves developing 'a personal philosophy of teaching';
- is about 'the enduring human struggle to "live out" educational values in practice';
- 'is a moral category – not about "what works" but about what is "good"';
- 'involves, at an institutional level, "vibrant, deliberative cultures" in which intellectual curiosity is supported and ideas and practices are shared and discussed rather than held to a fixed set of criteria';
- 'is found in the concrete circumstances that underpin teaching and learning, rather than in brilliant or "heroic" individuals';
- 'should be conceived as part of excellence in the whole of the academic life, and not in rivalry with or in distraction from research excellence'.

(Gunn & Fisk, 2013, p. 21, summarising Skelton, 2009, pp. 109–111)

This conception of teaching excellence, with its emphasis on teaching and learning as moral engagement, is one that seems to resonate with students and academics alike (Abbas, Brennan, Abbas, Gantogtokh, & Bryman, 2016; Bartram et al., 2019; Su & Wood, 2012).

CONCLUSION

Teaching excellence is a slippery and highly contested concept that remains at the centre of a dynamic, evolving area of debate. Both 'teaching' and 'excellence' are potentially problematic, the former encouraging a focus on the act of teaching and the latter sometimes shifting attention unduly towards innovation and exceptionalism. There are plenty of voices who argue that the sector should concentrate on raising the status and standard of teaching generally. Equally, teaching excellence and excellent student learning, though often connected, are not necessarily two sides of the same coin.

It is also worth noting the shift in the teaching excellence agenda. This is reflected in the distinction that is made between 'teaching excellence', pertaining to overall, system-wide conceptions of excellence, taking in what happens in and beyond the classroom, support structures and the curriculum in the broadest sense, and 'teacher excellence' which generally links to individual philosophies and practices. The former often subsumes the latter. Moreover, teaching excellence is rarely achieved in a vacuum and needs clear institutional policies and practices to sustain it.

Another way of characterising this shift is the move from 'surface excellence' – usually module-specific, resulting from individual enthusiasms or insights and often demonstrated in new, innovative, technologically rich initiatives, valorised in awards and rewards schemes – to 'deep excellence' – visible at programme or more usually institutional level and displaying systemic, embedded and everyday features: a combination of coherent values, sound structures and robust practices that are widely shared and even taken for granted. The former in practice tends to prioritise what happens in the classroom; the latter adopts a more holistic view beyond the classroom, encompassing a variety of student/tutor interactions, support structures and the curriculum. It is concerned with both the transformative and the more instrumental outcomes of higher education and takes in links with research and with wider institutional and sectoral priorities such as equity, diversity and inclusion.

The intersections of teaching excellence with other key drivers of change and development in HE are rarely identified in the literature. It would be valuable to log where and how teaching excellence links to policies and practices around widening participation, retention and success, student engagement and employability. Such work may raise questions around teaching excellence for whom? And how far notions of teaching excellence have kept pace with changes in the composition of the student body? In the words of Abbas et al. (2016), 'to what extent do different students require different pedagogic approaches and different measures of "teaching excellence"?' (p. 10). Inclusive practice needs to be a feature of excellent teaching to ensure that different student groups have opportunities to develop their full potential in higher education (Mountford-Zimdars et al., 2015). As Burke et al. (2015) note, a critical reimagining of teaching excellence would emphasise that 'excellence and equity are bound together' (p. 41).

More work also needs to be done to augment the evidence base around the disciplinary dimensions of teaching excellence. Generic conceptions of teaching excellence do not adequately account for the specific academic, cultural and professional practices associated with particular subject disciplines or disciplinary families. This is where students potentially experience teaching excellence. Greatbatch and Holland (2016) note growing 'interest in how students in different disciplines have differing expectations from their courses' (p. 4), but how this translates into perceptions and assessments of teaching excellence is unclear. Given the resilience of signature pedagogies and the strength of disciplinary affiliations revealed in the literature, the consensus often expressed about the importance of the subject-specific element of the TEF may be under threat unless urgent work is undertaken.

Much could also be learnt from research into how teaching excellence is defined and operationalised in other phases of education. It is striking and perhaps ironic that much of this complementary literature emanates from university (education) departments but struggles to breach seemingly impermeable internal and cross-sectoral barriers. Indeed, with notable exceptions (for example, Darian, 2016; Robson, Wall, & Lofthouse, 2013; Su & Wood, 2012), it is often easy to imagine, when reading the research literature, that higher education exists in a bubble and that its students appear (untutored) from nowhere. Issues of teaching excellence, individual and collective, have long been addressed by researchers and policymakers in the schools and further education sectors.

In higher education, the notion of teaching excellence, for all its problematic features, is widely viewed as valuable galvanising, aspirational force. There is broad-based support for the idea of giving teaching greater prominence in the activities of HE institutions and opening up teaching practices and relevant institutional policies to more scrutiny. Equally, advocates argue that the TEF, for all its controversies and complexities, is a valid and useful instrument for driving up the quality of teaching in HE. It 'marks a striking advance for the sector' (Husbands, 2017b) and 'assesses the things that higher education students care about: teaching quality, the learning environment that supports them; and employment and further study outcomes' (Hawkins, 2018). It focuses on student outcomes and, importantly, raises 'the profile of one of the most important things that all universities do: teaching' (Husbands, 2017b). Even more cautious commentators like Ashwin (2017) and Berger and Wild (2016) acknowledge the value of ensuring that students have access to more detailed information on the quality of their courses.

But teaching excellence remains an elastic and often elusive concept: is difficult to argue against, but at the same time highly controversial. At the heart of these debates is the tension between teaching excellence as a worthwhile aspiration and its use as a performative tool. This disjuncture between a widely held belief in excellent teaching or individual teaching excellence and concerns about the legitimacy and usefulness of the purposes to which the concept is being deployed is at the core of critiques of the TEF. Commenting on the dual (both positive and negative) responses of their academics, Bartram et al. (2019) locate 'the pivotal and dividing point' as being 'where TE moves from being a matter of individual aspiration embedded within a sense of collective professionalism, to an institutional marketing/management tool in a consumerist HE context' (p. 13). These concerns are overlain with the range of theoretical and practical worries about measurement and the use of data (e.g., Ashwin, 2017; Berger & Wild, 2016; O'Leary & Wood, 2018; Wood & Su, 2017).

More generally, there are fears that the creation of another ranking system simply reinforces existing inequalities in the sector, and that it does not serve the interests of disadvantaged students whose needs it was partly intended to address (Bathmaker et al., 2016; Husbands, 2017a). The current iteration of the TEF in some senses runs counter to the other strands of government policy which seek to tackle stalling social mobility, since it may not be in an institution's best 'medal' interests to have a strong widening participation focus or track record. It is perhaps significant that less than a third of TEF2 submissions explicitly mentioned widening participation of students in their accounts of support in learning (Moore et al., 2017). Equally, as the TEF Panel Chair noted, few TEF submissions 'were systematic on the ways in which disadvantage is addressed and how they close performance gaps among groups of students' (Husbands, 2017a).

The thrust of these critiques and those derived from some of the alternative perspectives outlined above suggests that rather than seeking singular definitions and conceptions, it may be more useful to talk of 'teaching excellences': to reflect a stratified and plural sector, a diverse student body and different discipline families. Bartram et al.'s (2019) respondents similarly argue against singularity, with one characterising teaching excellence as 'incorrigibly plural' (p. 13). A useful starting point to explore more pluralistic versions of teaching excellence would be to revisit Gunn and Fisk's (2013) taxonomy and the more holistic conceptions of teaching excellence proposed by a number of commentators from Gibbs (2008) and Skelton (2007; 2009) onwards. These emphasise the relational, emotional and moral dimensions of teaching, underpinned by cooperative principles and built on collegial practices.

Recent writers also seek to reconnect the concept of teaching excellence to the processes of learning and to notions of professionalism and authenticity. Wood and Su (2017), for example, suggest that 'we need a more nuanced inclusive interpretation of "teaching excellence" which recognises the conjoined nature of teaching and research in higher education, and also rebalances a focus on outcomes-related measures with understandings of purposes and development of the processes of learning' (p. 463). O'Leary and Wood (2018) similarly argue against the 'TEF's narrow conceptualisation of teaching excellence' and propose 'an alternative vision that seeks to reimagine excellence by integrating the complex, context-specific and collaborative characteristics of HE teaching into an approach that has authentic and meaningful improvement at its core, along with an ethos of professional responsibility' (p. 1).

As the TEF2 submissions and a host of recent studies confirm, teaching excellence is the focus of much frenetic activity and diligent research. It is also a topic that abounds with myths (Ashwin, 2016a) and no little wishful thinking. Yet, as this review also reveals, it is above all an arena for high aspirations and lofty ambitions for 'great teaching' to be seen as 'a virtuous and moral enterprise' (Su & Wood, 2012, p. 143). The key, as Ashwin (2016a) notes, is to ensure that we engage with teaching excellence 'in a way that is congruent with scholarly teaching practices'. From the Skills for Life initiative in the 2000s to SATs testing for 7-year-olds, the history of UK education is littered with initiatives that hit the target but miss the point. It remains to be seen whether the TEF, like the Olympics that its medal system mimics, becomes a periodic, time-constrained 'event' with defined end points and clear winners and losers or it transcends initial scepticism to become a truly developmental process that serves wider moral rather than narrow managerialist purposes.

REFERENCES

Abbas, A., Brennan, J., Abbas, J., Gantogtokh, O., & Bryman, K. (2016). *Teaching excellence in the disciplines*. York: Higher Education Academy.

Ashwin, P. (2016, July 4). Reflective teaching and seven myths of teaching excellence. Keynote presentation presented at the UK Council for Graduate Education Annual Conference, Liverpool.

Ashwin, P. (2017). What is the teaching excellence framework, and will it work? *International Higher Education*, *88*, 10–11.

Ashwin, P., Abbas, A., & McLean, M. (2012). *Quality and inequality in undergraduate courses: A guide for national and institutional policy makers. Project Report.* Nottingham: University of Nottingham.

Barkas, L. A., Scott, J. M., Poppitt, N. J. & Smith, P. J. (2019). Tinker, tailor, policy-maker: Can the UK government's teaching excellence framework deliver its objectives? *Journal of Further and Higher Education, 43*(6), 801–813. doi:10.1080/0309877X.2017.1408789

Barnett, R. (2003). *Beyond all reason. Living with ideology in the university.* Buckingham: Society for Research into Higher Education & Open University Press.

Barnett, R. (2010). *Being a university.* London and New York, NY: Routledge.

Bartram, B., Hathaway, T., & Rao, N. (2019). 'Teaching excellence' in higher education: A comparative study of English and Australian academics' perspectives. *Journal of Further and Higher Education, 43*(9), 1284–1298. doi:10.1080/0309877X.2018.1479518

Bathmaker, A. M., Ingram, N., Abrahams, J., Hoare, A., Waller, R., & Bradley, H. (2016). *Higher education, social class and social mobility: The degree generation.* London: Palgrave Macmillan.

Berger, D., & Wild, C. (2016). The teaching excellence framework: Would you tell me, please, which way we ought to go from here? *Higher Education Review, 48*(3), 5–22.

BIS (Department for Business, Innovation and Skills). (2015). *Fulfilling our potential: Teaching excellence, social mobility and student choice.* London: BIS.

BIS (Department for Business, Innovation and Skills). (2016a). *Success as a knowledge economy: Teaching excellence, social mobility and student choice*. London: BIS.

BIS (Department for Business, Innovation and Skills). (2016b). *Teaching excellence framework technical consultation for year two*. London: BIS.

Blackmore, P., Blackwell, R., & Edmondson, M. (2016). Tackling wicked issues: Prestige and employment outcomes in the teaching excellence framework. HEPI Occasional Paper 14. HEPI, Oxford. Retrieved from https://www.hepi.ac.uk/wp-content/uploads/2016/09/Hepi_TTWI-Web.pdf

Brabon, B. (2016, May 19). Beyond the Rubicon: Exploring the TEF in the disciplines [blog post]. Retrieved from https://www.heacademy.ac.uk/blog/beyond-rubicon-exploring-tef-disciplines-dr-ben-brabon-hea

Brockerhoff, L., Stensaker, B., & Huisman, J. (2014). Prescriptions and perceptions of teaching excellence: A study of the national 'Wettbewerb Exzellente Lehre' initiative in Germany. *Quality in Higher Education, 20*(3), 235–254.

Brown, R., & Carasso, H. (2013). *Everything for sale? The marketisation of UK higher education*. London and New York, NY: Routledge.

Brusoni, M., Damian, R., Sauri, J. G., Jackson, S., Komurcugil, H., Malmedy, M., … Zobel, L. (2014). The concept of excellence in higher education. European Association for Quality Assurance in Higher Education (ENQA), Brussels. Retrieved from http://www.enqa.eu/index.php/publications/papers-reports/occasional-papers/

Burke, P. J., & Crozier, G. (2012). *Teaching inclusively: Challenging pedagogical spaces*. York: Higher Education Academy.

Burke, P. J., Stevenson, J., & Whelan, P. (2015). Teaching 'excellence' and pedagogic stratification in higher education. *International Studies in Widening Participation*, 2(2), 29–43.

Cashmore, A., Cane, C. & Cane, R. (2013). Rebalancing promotion in the HE sector: Is teaching excellence being rewarded? Higher Education Academy, York. Retrieved from https://www.heacademy.ac.uk/system/files/hea_reward_publication_rebalancingpromotion_0.pdf

Clegg, S. (2007). The demotic turn: Excellence by fiat. In A.-Skelton (Ed.), *International perspectives on teaching excellence in higher education: Improving knowledge and practice* (pp. 91–102) Abingdon: Routledge.

Coe, R., Aloisi, C., Higgins, S., & Major, L. E. (2014). *What makes great teaching? Review of the underpinning research*. Durham: Sutton Trust/University of Durham.

Courtney, S. (2016, May 17). How the TEF could spread round the world [blog post]. Retrieved from https://www.heacademy.ac.uk/blog/how-tef-could-spread-around-world-dr-steven-j-courtney-university-manchester

Darian, L. (2016). *Designing a teaching excellence framework: Lessons from other sectors*. Oxford: HEPI.

De Courcy, E. (2015). Defining and measuring teaching excellence in higher education in the 21st century. *The College Quarterly*, *18*(1), 1–6.

DfES (Department for Education and Skills) (2003). *The Future of higher education (Cm5735)*. London: HMSO.

Dinetke, T., Dolmans, D., Wolfhagen, I., & Van Der Vleuten, C. (2004). The development and validation of a framework for teaching competencies in higher education. *Higher Education*, *48*(2), 253–268.

Evans, C. (2000). Against excellence. *Educational Developments*, *1*(2), 7.

Fitzmaurice, M. (2010). Considering teaching in higher education as a practice. *Teaching in Higher Education*, *15*(1), 45–55.

French, A. (2017). Contextualising excellence in higher education teaching: Understanding the policy landscape. In A. French & M. O'Leary (Eds.), *Teaching excellence in higher education: Challenges, changes and the teaching excellence framework* (pp. 5–38). Bingley: Emerald Publishing.

Gibbs, G. (2008). *Conceptions of teaching excellence underlying teaching award schemes*. York: Higher Education Academy.

Gibbs, G. (2010). *Dimensions of quality*. York: Higher Education Academy.

Gibson, R. (2007). Points of departure the art of creative teaching: Implications for higher education. *Teaching in Higher Education, 15*(5), 607–613.

Glasner, A. (2003). Can all teachers aspire to excellence? *Exchange*, *5*, 11. Retrieved from: www.exchange.ac.uk/issue5.asp

Greatbatch, D., & Holland, J. (2016). *Teaching quality in higher education: Literature review and qualitative research*. London: BIS.

Gunn, V., & Fisk, A. (2013). *Considering teaching excellence in higher education: 2007–2013. A literature review since the CHERI Report 2007.* York: Higher Education Academy.

Haggis, T. (2004). Meaning, identity and 'motivation': Expanding what matters in understanding learning in higher education? *Studies in Higher Education, 29*(3), 335–352.

Hammer, D., Piascik, P., Medina, M., Pittenger, A., Rose, R., Creekmore, F., … Steven, S. (2010). Recognition of teaching excellence. *American Journal of Pharmaceutical Education, 74,* 1–11.

Hawkins, Y. (2018, October 22). Subject-level TEF comes into sharper focus [Blog post]. Office for Students. Retrieved from https://www.officeforstudents.org.uk/news-blog-and-events/blog/subject-level-tef-comes-into-sharper-focus/.

HEA (Higher Education Academy). (2017). *HEA reflections on 'Evidencing teaching excellence'.* York: Higher Education Academy.

Healey, M., Flint, A., & Harrington, K. (2014). *Engagement through partnership: Students as partners in learning and teaching in higher education.* York: Higher Education Academy.

Henard, F., & Roseveare, D. (2012). *Fostering quality teaching in higher education.* Paris: OECD Institutional Management in Higher Education.

HEPI (Higher Education Policy Institute). (2016, February 25). Designing a teaching excellence framework: Lessons from other sectors [Press release]. Retrieved from https://www.hepi.ac.uk/2016/02/25/designing-a-teaching-excellence-framework-lessons-from-other-sectors-2/

Hubble, S., Foster, D. & Bolton, P. (2016). Higher Education and Research Bill, research briefing. Retrieved from http://researchbriefings.parliament.uk/ResearchBriefing/Summary/CBP-7608

Husbands, C. (2017a, June 22). Why ranking universities on graduate job prospects is a step in the right direction. *The Conversation*. Retrieved from https://theconversation.com/why-ranking-universities-on-graduate-job-prospects-is-a-step-in-the-right-direction-79962.

Husbands, C. (2017b, June 23). Universities, don't rest on your laurels - use the TEF to improve. *The Guardian*. Retrieved from https://www.theguardian.com/higher-education-network/2017/jun/23/universities-tef-improve.

John, P., & Fanghanel, J. (Eds.). (2015). *Dimensions of marketisation in higher education*. New York, NY and London: Routledge.

Johnson, J. (2015, July 1). Teaching at the heart of the system. Keynote address to Vice-Chancellors and sector leaders. London: UUK. Retrieved from https://www.gov.uk/government/speeches/teaching-at-the-heart-of-the-system

Kane, T. J., McCaffrey, D. F., Miller, T. & Staiger, D. O. (2013). Have we identified effective teachers? Validating measures of effective teaching using random assignment. Research Paper. MET Project. Bill & Melinda Gates Foundation, Seattle, DC.

Klemeric, M., & Ashwin, P. (2015). New directions for teaching, learning and student engagement in the European Higher Education Area. In R. Pricopie, P. Scott, J. Salmi, and A. Curaj (Eds.), *The future of higher education in Europe* (pp. 315–324). Dordrecht: Springer.

Knight, P. (2006). Book Reviews. *Studies in Higher Education, 31*(5), 637–650. doi:10.1080/03075070600923459

Land, R., & Gordon, G. (2015). *Teaching excellence initiatives: Modalities and operational factors.* York: Higher Education Academy.

Layton, C., & Brown, C. (2011). Striking a balance: Supporting teaching excellence award applications. *International Journal for Academic Development, 16*(2), 163–174.

Little, B., Locke, W., Parker, J., & Richardson, J. (2007). *Excellence in teaching and learning: A review of the literature for the higher education academy.* York: Higher Education Academy.

Locke, W. (2014). *Shifting academic careers: Implications for enhancing professionalism in teaching and supporting learning.* York: Higher Education Academy.

Lodge, M. L., & Bonsanquet, A. (2014). Evaluating quality learning in higher education: Re-examining the evidence. *Quality in Higher Education, 20*(1), 3–23.

Lubicz-Nawrocka, T., & Bunting, K. (2019). Student perceptions of teaching excellence: An analysis of student-led teaching award nomination data. *Teaching in Higher Education, 24*(1), 63–80 doi:10.1080/13562517.2018.1461620

Macfarlane, B. (2007). Beyond performance in teaching excellence. In A. Skelton (Ed.), *International perspectives on teaching excellence in higher education: Improving knowledge and practice* (pp. 48–59). Abingdon: Routledge.

McGhee, P. (2016, August 26). Will the Teaching Excellence Framework be a licence for universities to raise fees. *The Guardian.* Retrieved from https://www.theguardian.com/education/2016/aug/22/teaching-excellence-framework-universities-tuition-fees-tef.

Moore, J., Higham, L., Sanders, J., Jones, S., Candarli, D., & Mountford-Zimdars, A. (2017). *Evidencing teaching excellence: Analysis of the teaching excellence framework (TEF2) provider submissions*. York: Higher Education Academy.

Morley, L. (2003). *Quality and power in higher education*. Buckingham: Society for Research into Higher Education and Open University Press.

Mountford-Zimdars, A., Sabri, D., Moore, J., Sanders, J., Jones, S., & Higham, L. (2015). *Causes of differences in student outcomes*. Bristol: HEFCE.

National Committee of Inquiry into Higher Education (NCIHE). (1997). Higher education for a learning society. Dearing Report. HMSO, London.

Nixon, J. (2007). Excellence and the good society. In A. Skelton (Ed.), *International perspectives on teaching excellence in higher education: Improving knowledge and practice* (pp. 74–88). Abingdon: Routledge.

O'Leary, M., Cui, V., & French, A. (2019). *Understanding, recognising and rewarding teaching quality in higher education: An exploration of the impact and implications of the Teaching Excellence Framework*. London: University and College Union.

O'Leary, M., & Wood, P. (2018). Reimagining teaching excellence: Why collaboration, rather than competition, holds the key to improving teaching and learning in higher education. *Educational Review*, doi:10.1080/00131911.2019.1524203

Pring, R., Hayward, G., Hodgson, A., Johnson, J., Keep, E., Oancea, … Wilde, S. (2009). *Education for all*. London: Routledge.

QAA (Quality Assurance Agency). (2015). Higher education review: Second year findings 2014–2015. Gloucester, QAA.

Richards, C. (2015). More outstanding nonsense: A critique of Ofsted criteria. *FORUM, 57*(2), 233–238.

Robson, S., Wall, K., & Lofthouse, R. (2013). Raising the profile of innovative teaching in higher education? Reflections on the EquATE project. *International Journal of Teaching and Learning in Higher Education, 25*(1), 92–102.

Rostan, M., & Vaira, M. (Eds.). (2011). *Questioning excellence in higher education: Policies, experiences and challenges in national and comparative perspective*. Rotterdam: Sense.

Sabri, D. (2011). What's wrong with 'the student experience'? *Discourse: Studies in the Cultural Politics of Education, 32*(5), 657–667.

Shephard, K., Harland, T., Stein, S., & Tidswell, T. (2011). Preparing an application for a higher-education teaching-excellence award: Whose foot fits Cinderella's shoe? *Journal of Higher Education Policy and Management, 33*(1), 47–56.

Skelton, A. (2005). *Understanding teaching excellence in higher education: Towards a critical approach*. London: Routledge.

Skelton, A. (Ed.). (2007). *International perspectives on teaching excellence in higher education: Improving knowledge and practice*. Abingdon: Routledge.

Skelton, A. (2009). A 'teaching excellence' for the times we live in? *Teaching in Higher Education, 14*(1), 107–112.

Stevenson, J., Burke, P. J., Whelan, P., Sealey, P., & Ploner, J. (2014). *Pedagogic stratification and the shifting landscape of higher education*. York: Higher Education Academy.

Strang, L., Bélanger, J., Manville, C., & Meads, C. (2016). *Review of the research literature on defining and demonstrating quality teaching and impact in higher education*. York: Higher Education Academy.

Su, F., & Wood, M. (2012). What makes a good university lecturer? Students' perceptions of teaching excellence. *Journal of Applied Research in Higher Education, 4*(2), 142–155.

Taylor, C., & Robinson, C. (2012). Student engagement in higher education: Theory, context, practice. *Journal of Applied Research in Higher Education*, *4*(2), 90–92. doi: 10.1108/jarhe.2012.53304baa.001.

Torres, C. A. (2013). Neoliberalism as a new historical bloc: A Gramscian analysis of Neoliberalism's common sense in education. *International Studies in Sociology of Education*, *23*(2), 80–106.

Trigwell, K. (2010). Judging university teaching. *International Journal for Academic Development, 6*(1), 65–73. doi: 10.1080/13601440110033698

Trigwell, K. (2012). Relations between teachers' emotions in teaching and their approaches to teaching in higher education. *Instructional Science*, *40*(3), 607–621. doi:10.1007/s1125101191923

Trowler, V. (2010). *Student engagement literature review*. York: Higher Education Academy.

Wespel, J., Orr, D., & Jaegar, M. (2013). The implications of excellence in research and teaching. *International Higher Education*, *72*, 13–15.

Wood, M., & Su, F. (2017). What makes an excellent lecturer? Academics' perspectives on the discourse of 'teaching excellence' in higher education. *Teaching in Higher Education*, 22(4), 451–466.

Zhu, C., Wang, D., Cai, Y., & Engels, N. (2013). What core competencies are related to teachers' innovative teaching? *Asia-Pacific Journal of Teacher Education*, 41(1), 9–27. doi:10.1080/1359866X.2012.753984

2

OPERATIONALISING TEACHING EXCELLENCE IN HIGHER EDUCATION: FROM 'SHEEP-DIPPING' TO 'VIRTUOUS PRACTICE'

John Sanders, Joanne Moore, and Anna Mountford-Zimdars

ABSTRACT

This chapter critically engages with ways that teaching excellence has been operationalised in practice. Specific focus is on developing individual teaching excellence, rewarding of success and recognition of teaching excellence and the building of evidence around what works in teaching for the benefits of students. We consider the daily interactions with students that form the basis of frameworks of teaching excellence before arguing that operationalisations of teaching excellence are highly context specific and operate at the level of institutions and the whole higher education sector. We discuss the criteria that underpin teaching excellence awards. This includes governance as well as development frameworks. After considering the complex links between research and teaching and the importance of the disciplinary dimension of teaching excellence, the chapter finally looks at the skills and attributes commonly associated with individual teacher excellence and argues that these are exceptionally difficult to pin down let alone measure. It concludes with some reflections on some of the challenges faced by institutions as they seek to develop the quality of teaching whilst meeting the requirements of the TEF.

Keywords: Individual excellence; measurement; frameworks; awards; recognition; institution

INTRODUCTION

Mechanisms for developing teaching excellence in the HE sector have tended to be based on three interlinked prongs: firstly, initiatives focused on building individual capability through professional development type work with staff members; secondly, the rewarding of success/recognition of excellence when it is seen to happen and thirdly, initiatives with a focus on building the evidence around pedagogy that works to improve the educational experiences and results in benefits for students (however measured). These aspects operate both within institutions and at the level of the sector as a whole. Fig. 2.1 provides a visual summary of these key strands and the constituent aspects and processes by which teaching excellence is currently operationalised. It is worth noting, in addition, that the effectiveness of the levers to develop teaching excellence are impacted by wider sectoral structures and factors. For example, the frameworks in place for resourcing teaching and learning may limit or facilitate developments in teaching excellence and affect the capability

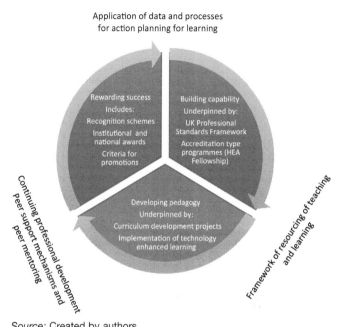

Application of data and processes
for action planning for learning

Rewarding success
Includes:
Recognition schemes
Institutional and
national awards
Criteria for
promotions

Building capability
Underpinned by:
UK Professional
Standards Framework
Accreditation type
programmes (HEA
Fellowship)

Developing pedagogy
Underpinned by:
Curriculum development projects
Implementation of technology
enhanced learning

Continuing professional development
Peer support mechanisms and
peer mentoring

Framework of resourcing of teaching
and learning

Source: Created by authors.

Fig. 2.1. Mechanisms for Teaching Excellence.

of HE staff to deliver excellence. Opportunities for training and support including sharing/peer approaches will facilitate the dissemination of excellence. There is also an increasing focus on the application of data in the identification of excellence (linked to the imperative that excellence should lead to student success).

This chapter focuses mainly on the first two of these strands – developing capability and rewarding success, though it touches on the third, pedagogy, through its consideration of the research-teaching nexus and the Scholarship of Teaching and Learning (SoTL). It draws on relevant research to explore how macro level imperatives to develop and demonstrate teaching excellence play out practically on the ground in institutions and in lecturers' daily interactions with students. The literature reviewed focuses mainly on UK higher education, though international evidence and research from other sectors of education are drawn on to illuminate particular aspects of the operationalisation of teaching excellence.

The chapter begins with a brief account of sectoral structures for developing individual capability and for providing professional recognition and how they support teaching excellence both directly and indirectly. It then examines ways in which teaching excellence is recognised and rewarded within universities; focussing in particular on the criteria that underpin teaching excellence awards (TEAs) and how such schemes are perceived and operationalised. After considering the complex links between research and teaching and the importance of the disciplinary dimension of teaching excellence, the chapter finally looks at the skills and attributes commonly associated with individual teacher excellence and argues that these are exceptionally difficult to pin down let alone measure. It concludes with some reflections on some of the challenges faced by institutions as they seek to develop the quality of teaching whilst meeting the requirements of the TEF.

BUILDING CAPABILITY AND SUPPORTING EXCELLENCE

An extensive range of literature has illuminated the wide spectrum of policies, processes and activities that have sought to enhance the status of teachers and provide recognition and reward for teaching excellence (see Land & Gordon, 2015, for an analytical international overview). Such initiatives include teaching fellowships and awards, promotion and reward systems, professional development opportunities and schemes for professional recognition. All have contributed directly or indirectly to the development of teaching excellence within the sector.

Ron Dearing's landmark report (NCIHE, 1997) included proposals to recognise and reward teaching. The subsequent creation of the Institute for Learning and Teaching (the forerunner for the Higher Education Academy [HEA]), the inauguration of the National Teaching Fellowship Scheme (NTFS), the articulation of the dimensions of professional practice in the UK Professional Standards Framework (UKPSF) and the later development of Centres of Excellence in Teaching and Learning (CETLs) in England and Northern Ireland all sought to operationalise this broad aim.

In addition, the early 2000s saw the production of institutional learning and teaching strategies that emphasised and supported teaching excellence (Gibbs & Habeshaw, 2002; HEA, 2005; see Little, Locke, Parker, & Richardson, 2007, p. 16). These were often implemented by institutional Education Development Centres that had a remit for enhancing the quality of teaching and learning and facilitating the professional development of staff. Recent years have seen the improvement of teaching and learning quality become an increasing priority (Jones & Wisker, 2012) and, since the advent of the TEF, a push to gain teaching qualifications like the Postgraduate Certificate in HE Learning and Teaching and associated accreditation such as HEA fellowship with some institutions setting specific 'professional recognition' targets (O'Leary, Cui & French, 2019, p. 76).

The HEA fellowship scheme has become a key mechanism for developing capability and enhancing teaching quality amongst HE staff (van der Sluis, Burden, & Huet, 2017). Although not explicitly concerned with individual teacher excellence, its underpinning processes and mentoring approaches can be viewed as indirectly supporting teaching excellence. As the TEF2 submissions demonstrated, the HEA fellowship scheme is well-embedded into the culture of HEIs (Moore et al., 2017) with many using it as an indicator of a commitment to excellence.

The UKPSF was created to set out the expectations of what professional practice in higher education looks like. Its four-level sector-wide framework of professional recognition and accreditation, ranging from Associate Fellow to Principal Fellow, provides some implicit descriptors for teaching excellence. It is an important tool for teacher development and underpins the HEA fellowship scheme, though some have argued that it lacks a clear alignment with the realities of career development and progression in higher education (Turner et al., 2013).

The now defunct CETLs, in contrast, had a stronger institutional and departmental focus, but the clarity of the original policy intentions suffered somewhat through being 'lost in translation' (Turner & Gosling, 2012). Funding for the 74 locally based centres was not mainstreamed, and their impact in relation to articulating a clear notion of teaching excellence was muted (Land & Gordon, 2015; Turner & Gosling, 2012).

The NTFS (launched in 2000) focuses on individual teacher development and the creation of a community of best practice and sector leadership. Initial evaluations of the scheme noted its individualised, psychologised and performative features and its (perhaps excessive) focus on innovatory delivery methods (Skelton, 2004). Botterill's (2013) report, for example, confirms that National Teaching Fellows were 'very effective in delivering innovative projects' (p. 12). Rickinson, Spencer and Stainton's (2012) review of the scheme is largely positive and notes how institutions see it as a marker of teaching excellence and sometimes have embedded it into their promotion policies. However, this study also lists lack of clarity in the nomination and assessment process, insufficient focus on 'real teachers' and lack of alignment with the UKPSF amongst its weaknesses.

RECOGNITION AND REWARD

At the institutional level, the implementation of these national schemes and frameworks has been matched by the more explicit inclusion of teaching excellence within institutional reward and promotion systems. Skelton (2005), for example, highlights the importance of the formal recognition of teaching in promotions procedures and the introduction of teaching-related promotions to new posts, in nurturing an institutional culture of excellence. Meanwhile, Gibbs and Habeshaw (2002) pondered whether different 'levels of excellence' were required for different levels of promotion (p. 6). They also note the danger of generic criteria for teaching excellence and promotion tending to privilege traditional forms of pedagogy and discourage risk-taking.

The recognition and reward of teaching excellence within promotion systems has continued to grow, albeit distributed unevenly. Cashmore, Cane, and Cane (2013), for example, chart significant progress in the incorporation of teaching excellence criteria in universities' reward and recognition policies, and O'Leary et al. (2019) report 'more opportunities to gain promotion/career progression via a teaching route' since the advent of the TEF (p. 5). However, Cashmore et al. (2013) also note a gap between policy and implementation and outline some of the challenges faced by institutions seeking to reflect the new prominence of teaching in promotion pathways and systems at a time when academic roles are becoming more diverse (Graham, 2015).

The primacy of publication, identified by D'Andrea and Gosling (2005) and Young (2006), remains a resilient feature of promotion systems even when institutional policies are formally in place to reward both teaching and research (Robinson & Hilli, 2016). Similarly, writing from a research-intensive university perspective, Robson, Wall and Lofthouse (2013) note academics' scepticism about fundamental change when 'promotion applications citing teaching excellence require evidence of engagement with pedagogic research' (p. 92). This remains a challenge, one that Graham (2016) meets head-on in her comprehensive template for evaluating teaching achievement in engineering.

More generally, Gunn and Fisk (2013) argue that teaching-focussed and research-focussed reward and recognition structures need to be aligned and integrated more explicitly (p. 12). Excellence is increasingly used in reward and recognition schemes to differentiate higher-level teaching from threshold quality teaching. However, for Gunn and Fisk (2013), the absence of agreed definitions or conceptions of what teaching excellence is means that there are inevitably differences and tensions between locally determined (discipline/department) reward and recognition methods and criteria developed or interpreted centrally or institutionally – a feature commented on by some of the Social Science deans in Abbas, Brennan, Abbas, Gantogtokh and Bryman (2016) study.

TEACHING EXCELLENCE AWARDS

The development and spread of TEAs is another manifestation of the multilevel and multifaceted movement to enhance the status and recognition of teaching. It is also a place where the distinction between 'good' and 'excellent' teaching emerges and an arena within which the contested nature of the notion of teaching excellence is played out. A variety of TEAs, their underpinning assumptions and criteria and the people who won them are discussed in an extensive literature (see D'Andrea, 2007; Devlin & Samarawickrema; 2010, Gibbs, 2008; Hammer et al., 2010; Layton & Brown, 2011; Leibowitz, van Schalkwyk, Ruiters, Farmer, & Adendorff, 2012: Olsson & Roxa, 2013; Skelton, 2005). Recent international additions include Shephard, Harland, Stein, and Tidswell's (2011) study of 10 award winners from five different countries, Brockerhoff et al.'s (2014) account of the institutionally focussed Competition for Teaching Excellence in Germany and Land and Gordon's (2015) valuable multination overview.

Gunn and Fisk (2013) provide a succinct summary of this broad international material (pre-2013) and of the criteria underpinning TEAs. They note the 'wide divergences in the purposes and processes of teaching awards' (p. 24), ranging from the recognition and celebration of individual excellence to broader ambitions to promote and disseminate excellent practice. Their analysis also highlights four central themes of TEAs (relating to key areas of practice): planning and delivery; assessment; evaluation and reflection and contribution to the profession (p. 25, Diagram 4). They note that 'planning and delivery' (what teachers do in delivering their programmes/courses) are particularly strongly represented in the criteria, reflecting the 'performance' approach to teaching excellence noted by Macfarlane (2011).

Student-led teaching awards (SLTAs), based on the nominations or votes of students, and student-led components in broader schemes have become a common feature of teacher excellence awards in recent years. For example, the award panel for the NTFS included student members for the first time in 2016. SLTAs, which began as a collaborative venture between NUS and HEA in Scotland in 2009 and which were conceived as a vehicle for simultaneously raising the profile of teaching and celebrating best practice, have spread across the United Kingsom (see, Lubicz-Nawrocka & Bunting, 2019). Their reception has been mixed. Madriaga and Morley's (2016) study of staff perceptions of an institutional SLTA scheme, for example, reveals the tensions between its public and its private face and highlights the interplay between teachers' desire for their craft to be recognised and valued by their institution and their doubts about whether something as intangible, ambiguous and multidimensional as teaching excellence can be properly captured in an annual ritual.

More broadly, Gunn and Fisk (2013) note that critics have argued that SLTAs run the risk of becoming little more than popularity or charisma contests and have come to symbolise a consumerist view of higher education – 'neoliberal rubbish' in the pithy summary of one respondent to Madriaga and Morley's (2016) staff survey. The tendency of such schemes to link excellent teaching to 'on-stage' performance (Macfarlane, 2007) and encourage the 'entertainment' model of teaching (McCulloch, 2009) is also cited. In addition, doubts about students' ability to discern teaching excellence are voiced in a number of sources (Davies, Hope, & Robertson, 2012; Macfarlane, 2007; Madriaga & Morley, 2016), and, certainly, a limited conception of teaching (mainly equated with lecturing) was revealed in Thompson and Zeitzeva's (2012) analysis of student nominations.

However, the same study dispels the 'popularity myth'. Equally, a more sophisticated student evaluation of excellent teacher attributes is revealed in other research (Davies et al., 2012; Foster & Southwell-Sander, 2014; Lubicz-Nawrocka & Bunting, 2019). The two latter studies also make a more general point about the role of SLTAs in fostering a culture of partnership. As Gunn and Fisk (2013) note, new participative approaches to student engagement have the potential to aid the redefinition of teaching excellence (p. 36). This is supported by Lubicz-Nawrocka and Bunting's (2019) conclusion that students' prioritisation of the 'critical' and 'moral' dimensions of teaching excellence 'suggests the important role that student-staff partnerships can play in enhancing teaching and learning' (p. 76).

The practical impact of the teaching awards culture in enhancing teaching, and ameliorating its status as the 'poor relation' of research (Young, 2006), has been the subject of much debate in the literature. Some commentators note the developmental benefits to recipients and the role of awards in recognising the achievements of dedicated individuals (Skelton, 2009). Others emphasise their potential divisiveness (Gibbs, 2012), 'spurious objectivity' (Gibbs, 2007) and the lack of evidence from evaluation reports of improvements of teaching standards (Skelton, 2007, quoted in Skelton, 2009, p. 110). Gunn and Fisk (2013) conclude that little has changed since Gibbs (2008) noted that in TEAs, individual excellence is primarily defined by 'initiatives and individuals which *have come to be recognised* as excellent, rather than as having been identified through theoretically robust, systematic or strategic models' (p. 47).

Another possible objection to the awards culture is that it smacks of tokenism (Evans, 2000) and excessive individualism. Sensitivity to this accusation may in part explain the HEA's development of the Collaborative Award for Teaching Excellence (CATE) to sit alongside the NTFS scheme (HEA, 2016). Other new awards are aligned not to disciplines but generic themes (e.g., employability, student engagement), signalling a shift away from individuals to teams.

Finally, the awards culture runs the risk of allocating heroic status to everyday activities and expected attributes, thereby reflecting an inflationary feature of modern culture that lionises people for simply doing their job (whether they be nurses, soldiers or teachers). Such a conception is implied in the very title of the 'Teaching Heroes' campaign in Ireland. Led by the National Forum for the Enhancement of Teaching and Learning in Higher Education, this student-led initiative aims to identify and celebrate 'impactful teachers' (National Forum, 2016). Indeed, Gunn and Fisk (2013) identify 'heroic individuals' as one of the key recurring themes in the literature around teaching excellence and higher education teaching leadership (p. 43). However, Skelton (2009) perceptively warns that 'we should not look for teaching excellence as an essence within heroic individuals' (p. 110).

SCHOLARSHIP AND THE RESEARCH-TEACHING NEXUS

The links between research and teaching in higher education are multifarious and rarely operate in simple mechanistic ways (Trowler & Wareham, 2007). Neither are they automatic. Jenkins, Healey, and Zetter (2007, p. 17) quote Hattie and Marsh's (1996) conclusion that the idea that research and teaching are 'intrinsically linked is an enduring myth'. Equally, the benefits of being taught by leading researchers have proved difficult to demonstrate (Blackmore, 2009, cited in Hay, Weller, & Ashton, 2015, p. 25). In practice, research-related teaching can be research-led, research-orientated or research-based (Jenkins et al., 2007, pp. 28–29) or even lead researcher-based (Hay et al., 2015). Gunn and Fisk (2013), noting the surge in discussion about research–teaching linkages, attribute it not only to external policy pressures including the challenge to the supremacy of research-based higher education but also to internal institutional dynamics and the desire to reintegrate academic roles (p. 43).

The close link between research and teaching within the 'research-teaching nexus' (Gunn & Fisk, 2013) or (if you prefer) the 'teaching-research nexus' (Jenkins et al., 2007; Little et al., 2007) is often cited as an important dimension of teaching excellence. In particular, notions of scholarship are frequently linked to excellent teaching. An extensive discrete literature has grown up around the concept of the SoTL (Fanghanel, Pritchard, Potter, & Wisker, 2015). With its focus on teaching and learning strategies that underpin the curriculum and promote research-informed learning, SoTL is frequently cited as a key feature of teaching excellence (see Gale, 2007; Roxå, Olsson, & Mårtensson, 2008), or in criteria for institutional awards or promotion (reward and recognition) systems.

However, as Gunn and Fisk (2013) point out, it can also be subject to 'research framework' pressures and distorting tendencies. Moreover, the evidence that scholars of teaching are excellent teachers is not conclusive. To paraphrase the analogy used by Little et al. (2007), knowledge of how a car engine works does not necessarily make you a good driver (p. 19). More generally, the literature suggests that individual teacher excellence can be attained without systematic engagement in scholarship or theory, but teaching excellence as a dynamic institutional or departmental feature is unlikely to be sustained without serious engagement in SoTL.

The research-teaching nexus also takes in teaching that is closely informed by the latest research or by research-based approaches (see, for example, Bartram, Hathaway, & Rao, 2019). Some of the literature argues that student experiences and outcomes are enhanced by encouraging a culture of inquiry and actively engaging in research-teaching activities (Brew, 2007; Jenkins & Healey, 2007) and by the coproduction of knowledge (Healey & Jenkins, 2009). This is supported by examples from Scotland (QAA, 2008), Wales

(Colley & Healey, 2012) and Ireland (Murphy, Griffen & Higgs, 2010). Such teaching methods are often highlighted in prescriptions for high-quality teaching, for example, in the humanities and social sciences, and they align with the ambitions expressed by social science deans in Abbas et al.'s (2016) study to develop 'critical and interactive academic engagement' amongst their students. For Neary (2016), research-engaged teaching 'is not just a teaching technique, but is part of a broader debate about the meaning and purpose of higher education' (p. 692).

Excellent teaching in relation to the research-teaching nexus is defined in part by an ability to develop curricula focused less on syllabus content and more on nurturing research-like attributes (in students) or being a researcher (Gunn & Fisk, 2013, p. 13). However, the extent to which this is possible may depend on the nature of the subject and its research traditions, the level of knowledge required and the different ways in which staff see knowledge in their disciplines. As Jenkins et al. (2007) note, 'disciplinary communities [may] differ in their attitudes to the roles of research in relationship to their teaching' (p. 35). They also conclude that, although student awareness of research culture is higher at research-intensive universities, type of institution (research-intensive or not) does not impact on students' actual experience of research. More generally, Skelton (2009) argues that 'the encouragement of different interconnections between teaching and research (SoTL, 'teaching-led' research and 'research-informed' teaching) may all help to bring teaching and research into closer relationship and support a holistic notion of excellence' (p. 111).

Again, though, there are dangers that, by reinforcing the notion of research as the highest calling, such conceptualisations of teaching excellence may be skewed towards teacher self-replication rather than addressing the needs of a diverse student body. This may provide part of the explanation why some students find it hard to sign up to the academic project (Mountford-Zimdars et al., 2015, p. 33); why (in relation to academic writing and assessment) they are put off by assessment and feedback practices that 'operate in exclusive ways' (Burke & Crozier, 2012, p. 38) or, more prosaically, why they find some academic skills like referencing, which mimic research-orientated approaches, so problematic (Sanders, 2010).

DISCIPLINARY DIMENSIONS

As we have seen above, in relation to the research-teaching nexus, the traditions and practices of different disciplinary communities can impact on how excellent teaching is conceptualised and operationalised. In addition, subject expertise is frequently cited as a key aspect of 'good', 'great' or 'outstanding' teaching (see Tables 2.1 and 2.2 below) and provides a common touchstone for describing and understanding teaching excellence for academics (Bartram et al., 2019; Yarkova & Cherp, 2013). However, despite the proliferation of studies of disciplinary cultures and their potential impact on learning (Gunn, 2013; Kreber, 2009; Välimma & Ylijoki, 2010), Gunn and Fisk (2013) found surprisingly 'little research literature on how excellence in teaching is defined and operationalised from disciplinary perspectives' (p. 36), a conclusion echoed by Bartram et al. (2019, p. 3).

This is regrettable since, as Brabon (2016) notes, 'the day-to-day experience of the majority of teaching is grounded in the programme of study. Excellent teaching…is experienced and gauged locally and individually within a subject context' (p. 1). For Ashwin (2017), 'quality resides at the level of particular programs rather than institutions' (p. 11).

Correspondingly, Abbas et al. (2016) recommend that 'conceptions or measures of good teaching should take into account the knowledge-specific/disciplinary specific nature of what students gain from attending university' (p. 89). This view is echoed in proposals for the subject-level TEF and its ambitions to provide teaching excellence ratings at the subject level.

The subject discipline community is where an academic's sense of identity is generally forged (Becher & Trowler, 2001; Potter, 2008) and where their key loyalties lie. As Becher and Trowler (2001) work on 'academic tribes and territories' attests, such deep-rooted disciplinary differences impact significantly on how 'aspects of research and teaching are conceptualised, organised and communicated' (quoted in, Little et al., 2007, p. 24). American research into 'disciplinary signature pedagogies' similarly argues that distinctive disciplinary assumptions, underpinned by particular ways of knowing and ways of being, shape teaching and learning practices in the disciplines (see also, Cleaver, Lintern, & McLinden, 2014).

Correspondingly, notions of quality and understandings of excellence will necessarily vary according to the particular epistemological, cultural and pedagogical assumptions of different subject discipline communities (Greatbatch & Holland, 2016; Henard & Roseveare, 2012; Parpala, Lindblom-Ylänne, & Rytkönen, 2011). Abbas et al.'s (2016) report for HEA on 'teaching excellence in the disciplines' depicts a complex ecosystem in which 'a wide variety of discipline identities are at play in a highly rich and diverse sector' (p. 4). Although providing valuable insights into possible shared pedagogic identities, the survey also paints a picture of a complex environment in which the precise iteration of generic pedagogic aims might vary according to institutional setting, disciplinary context and Becher's (1989) typology of four disciplinary groupings (hard pure, soft pure, hard applied and soft applied). This all suggests that implementing a meaningful subject-level TEF will face significant challenges.

The research literature also provides some evidence of countervailing trends such as the blurring of boundaries, the weakening of disciplinary cultures and traditions and challenges to the primacy of academic disciplines as the basic organisational and intellectual units of HEIs (noted in Abbas et al., 2016; Bergseth, Petocz, & Abrandt Dahlgren, 2014; Chick, Haynie, & Guring, 2009; Skelton, 2009). Nevertheless, it remains important, especially given the hopes invested in the subject-level TEF, to understand how 'academics inhabit their disciplinary spaces' and how this 'influences the way that they engage with notions of teaching excellence' (Gunn & Fisk, 2013, p. 47).

INDIVIDUAL TEACHING EXCELLENCE: CHECKLISTS AND COMPARISONS

Ashwin, Abbas, and McLean (2012) argue that 'good teaching is vital if students are to engage with academic knowledge in transformative ways' (p. 2) – a conclusion supported by evidence from other sectors. Hanushek (2010), for example, shows how 'quality teachers are the key ingredient to a successful school and to improved student attainment' (p. 82), and McKnight, Graybeal Yarbro, and Graybeal (2016) cite Barber and Mourshed's (2007) dictum that 'the quality of an education system cannot exceed the quality of its teachers' (p. 2).

Identifying examples of excellent teaching practice is not straightforward. O'Leary and Wood (2018) warn of the dangers of focusing on 'public exercises in showcasing manufactured manifestations of excellence' (p. 15). Everyday eminence and mundane mastery rarely feature in peer-reviewed articles or teaching excellence nominations. Equally, an analysis of TEF2 submissions notes how the concepts of excellence and innovation can become subtly elided (Moore et al., 2017). In general, inventive course designs, novel approaches to teaching and the use of new technology tend to be overrepresented, whilst quotidian quality is sometimes overlooked.

This section focuses primarily on individual teaching excellence rather than system-wide or institutional concep-tions of teaching excellence. It takes in the psychologised notions of teaching excellence explored by Little at al. (2007) and includes a strong emphasis on the active participation by students in the learning environment, a key feature of some of the studies highlighted in Bryson's (2014) overview of student engagement. For Wood and Su (2017), 'the excellent teacher' is

> *...someone who is 'dedicated' and 'committed', able to establish motivational learning relationships, has expertise in their subject discipline and is skilled in pedagogic approaches that encourage learner independence and critical thought. The excellent teacher influences learners such that they develop the desire to learn and experience 'safe' learning spaces where they can try out ideas, share thinking, make mistakes, innovate and experiment.*

(pp. 461, 462)

The literature in relation to individual teaching excellence is extensive (especially when transnational or international research is included) but is mainly descriptive of particular approaches or initiatives rather than being empirically based or using comparator groups. An exception from the schools sector is Coe et al.'s (2014) analysis of over 200 pieces of research, which lists in descending order of evidence of impact on student outcomes 'six components of great teaching'.

A similar synthesis has yet to be done in relation to teaching excellence in higher education, though the literature here is useful in suggesting key themes or items for checklists that articulate possible dimensions of teaching excellence for individual academics. In an Australian context, for example, Devlin and Samarawickrema's (2010) reworking of the Australian Learning and Teaching Council's criteria highlights a range of desirable teacher attributes. This list echoes a number of the headings identified in Gunn and Fisk's (2013) summary of the recurring themes within the 'planning and delivery' category of criteria within TEAs.

These lists are summarised in Table 2.1 along with the four main characteristics of excellent teachers identified in Foster and Southwell-Sander's (2014) analysis of student nominations for an Outstanding Teacher Award and the five leading qualities that students (in another institutional award scheme) associated with inspirational teaching (Bradley, Kirby, & Madriaga, 2015). Taken together, they illustrate various combinations of cognitive and affective characteristics that are deemed to comprise individual teaching excellence. Unsurprisingly, the lists highlight the importance of discipline-related personal attributes such as detailed subject and curriculum knowledge alongside the teaching skills needed to manage diverse learning encounters. They also illuminate Gunn and Fisk's (2013) contention that such excellence is built on two core conditions: 'being dynamically engaged in teaching practice and inspiring and practically scaffolding the potential dynamic engagement of one's students' (p. 23). They also emphasise the relational and emotional dimensions of excellent teaching.

Table 2.1. Excellent/Effective/Inspirational Teachers and Teaching: HE-based Frameworks and Research.

Key Criteria under the 'Planning and Delivery' Theme within Teaching Excellence Awards (International)	Suggested Revisions to List of Skills and Practices of Effective Teaching for Individual Academics (Australia)	Characteristics of Excellent Teachers in an Analysis of Student Nominations for an Outstanding Teacher Award (UK University)	Leading Qualities of Inspirational Teachers in an Analysis of Student Comments in a Student-Led Award Scheme (UK University)
• Curriculum design: up-to-date knowledge of the discipline and appropriate learning outcomes. • Knowledge of the subject, including depth, breadth and challenge. • Ability to inspire and motivate.	• Facilitates student engagement. • Develops curriculum that demonstrates mastery of the field and anticipates students' future needs. • Fosters independent learning through	• Enthusiastic, engaging and challenging teaching. • Cares about and is accessible to students. • Good feedback and guidance. • Good subject knowledge.	• Enthusiasm for teaching and the subject, academically stimulating with up-to-date knowledge. • Pushes student to achieve their full potential. • Approachable and empathetic.

• Respect and care for students as individuals: diverse needs and respect for equality and diversity. • Active and group learning; using methods that foster engagement and participation. • Critical and scholarly: attitudes, attributes and understandings. • Engagement in assessment: diverse and appropriate feedback.	approaches to assessment and feedback. • Is respectful of both individual student needs and broader equality and diversity agendas. • Undertakes SoTL as 'active evaluation' for enhancing practice. • Engages with changing technologies.	• Positive attitude to students. • Understanding and supportive.
(Gunn & Fisk, 2013, p. 30)	(Devlin & Samarawickrema, 2010, in Gunn & Fisk, 2013, p. 23) (Foster & Southwell-Sander, 2014)	(Bradley et al., 2015)

Source: Created by authors.

A similar mix of qualities is revealed in Su and Wood's (2012) study of student perceptions of 'what makes a good university lecturer' (drawing on evidence from four HEA subject centres). This emphasises 'the lecturer's subject knowledge, willingness to help and inspirational teaching methods' (p. 142). Most of the generic attributes highlighted in Table 2.1 also chime with the findings of Bartram et al.'s 2019 study of English and Australian lecturers' conceptions of what constitutes teacher excellence. This revealed 'a vision of excellence based on high levels of staff-student interaction, engagement and personal involvement, supported by a commitment to subject knowledge and HE teaching/ professional development' (p. 12). In particular, respondents stressed the importance of facilitative, interactive pedagogy – a feature highlighted in both Abbas et al.'s (2016) sector-wide study and Revell and Wainwright's (2009) single institution investigation of what makes a geography lecture 'unmissable'.

Su and Wood (2012) importantly emphasise the value of sharing insights across different 'phases of learning'; and it is instructive to compare the HE table with the key themes emerging from Table 2.2 This lists Coe et al.'s (2014) 'components of great [school] teaching', alongside the results from a survey of stakeholders in England who were asked about the qualities of effective teachers (McKnight et al., 2016). It also includes Daw and Robinson's (2013) account of 'the common characteristics demonstrated by excellent teachers in their classrooms' (McAleavy, 2013) and Sammons, Kington, Lindorff-Vijayendran and Ortega's (2016) listing of the most common 'features of inspiring practice'. A number of these themes are also echoed in the 'attributes of effective teachers' discussed in Schleicher's (2016) international survey of the knowledge, skills and character qualities that successful (school) teachers require. It is notable that, whilst affective attributes and practical skills dominate the lists based mainly

Table 2.2. Great/Effective/Excellent/Inspiring Teachers and Teaching: Schools-based Research.

Six Components of Great Teaching that Show Evidence of Impact on Student Outcomes (Based on a Review of the Research)	The Top Six Qualities of Effective Teachers (Based on the Views of Stakeholders: Students, Parents, Teachers, Researchers and Administrators)	Five Characteristics Demonstrated by Excellent Teachers in Their Classrooms on a day-to-day Basis (Based on Teacher observations)	Eight Features of Inspiring Teaching (Based on Practitioner-led and Academic-led Studies of Classroom practice)
• Pedagogical content: deep knowledge of the subject and understanding of the ways students think about content. • Quality of instruction: including effective questioning and use of assessment.	• Ability to develop trusting, productive relationships and to relate to students. • Patient, kind and caring personality. • Ability to engage students in the course content and learning and motivate them to learn.	• Ability to respond and adapt planned lessons to meet the needs of learners. • Pedagogical subject knowledge that recognises how to engage students with the subject. • Ability to relate to students, recognise them as	• Lesson structures and activities: timings and transitions, differentiation, making connections. • Questioning and feedback: positive feedback, open-ended questions and circulation.

Table 2.2. (Continued)

Six Components of Great Teaching that Show Evidence of Impact on Student Outcomes (Based on a Review of the Research)	The Top Six Qualities of Effective Teachers (Based on the Views of Stakeholders: Students, Parents, Teachers, Researchers and Administrators)	Five Characteristics Demonstrated by Excellent Teachers in Their Classrooms on a day-to-day Basis (Based on Teacher observations)	Eight Features of Inspiring Teaching (Based on Practitioner-led and Academic-led Studies of Classroom practice)
• Classroom climate: high quality of interactions and high teacher expectations. • Classroom management: efficient use of lesson time, coordination of resources and management of students' behaviour. • Teacher beliefs: particular practices, purposes and	• Subject matter knowledge: expertise in subject area and curriculum knowledge. • Knowledge of learners: understanding the cognitive, social and emotional development of learners. • Professionalism: displaying appropriate professional knowledge, practices and	individual learners and make learning relevant to their lives and concerns. • Ability to strike the right balance between teacher input and independent learning. • Ability to judge the pace of the lesson and allow time for reflection.	• Classroom management: clear routines, responsibilities and mutual support. • Pupil behaviours: engagement, enthusiasm and task-focused talk. • Relationships/interactions: high expectations, supportive, respect, humour and enthusiasm.

theories that teachers hold/apply.
- Professional behaviours: e.g., CPD, reflection on practice, supporting colleagues and communicating with parents.

(Coe, Aloisi, Higgins, & Major, 2014)

behaviours in the workplace.

(McKnight et al., 2016)

(Daw & Robinson, 2013)

- Classroom environment: stimulating physical environment.
- Climate for learning: relaxed respectful, purposeful, fun.
- Teacher subject knowledge.

(Sammons, Kington, Lindorff-Vijayendran, & Ortega, 2016)

Source: Created by authors.

on stakeholder perceptions and observed practice, deep knowledge of subject content and curriculum is ever present and heads the research-based assessment of 'components of great teaching'.

As the headings for the tables make clear, these schemas rarely seek to differentiate excellent from merely good, effective or successful teaching. The durability or combination of qualities may be a key delineating factor in this regard. For Gunn and Fisk (2013),

> *...the applied research literature on teaching excellence suggests that an excellent teacher is one who is both dynamically engaged in practice and inspires dynamic engagement by their students, more or less permanently (or at least consistently over a period of a career).*

(p. 23)

Similarly, in relation to the schools sector, Coe et al. (2014) note that

> *...good teaching will likely involve a combination of these attributes [the six components of great teaching] manifested at different times; the very best teachers are those that demonstrate all of these features.*

(p. 2)

There are, however, dangers in reductionist approaches that seek to summarise the 'complex and diverse amalgam' that makes up the 'multi-faceted nature of teaching excellence' within simple checklists or mnemonics (Bartram et al., 2019, p. 9; Su & Wood, 2012). The outcome is liable to be CPD that results (in the memorable phrase of one Institute for Learning report) in staff being '"sheep-dipped" so that boxes could be ticked' (quoted in Thompson & Wolstencroft, 2014, p. 265). As numerous commentators across sectors have emphasised, teaching and learning are often intangible and occasionally mysterious processes that defy simple categorisation.

Finally, it is important to stress that individual teaching excellence, however articulated, is not achieved in a vacuum. The interaction of policies and practices at meso and micro levels is crucial (Gibbs, 2008). As Skelton, (2005) notes, 'however excellent an individual teacher appears to be, their work is always located in a broader institutional context' (p. 73). The factors that bolster excellent teaching and support successful learning are manifold and include key structural features, policies and practices, resources and libraries and study and pastoral support staff. What really counts is 'staff-student ratios; general infrastructure; conditions of work and secure contracts; time to reflect within the working day; and professional development opportunities' (Skelton, 2009, p. 110). Fanghanel (2007) similarly points out that 'teaching excellence is as much about systematic concepts of excellence equating to "excellent environments" as excellent (heroic even) individuals' (quoted in Gunn & Fisk, 2013, p. 37; see also Brusoni et al., 2014). 'Going the extra mile' may be dependent on whether or not you have already done a marathon.

Just as 'deep learning' can be encouraged by effective well-supported teachers operating in discipline-specific ways (Entwistle, 2009), so 'deep excellence' can be enabled by well-supported institutional policies and practices. This accords with findings from the schools sector which connect teachers' sense of self-efficacy (and their commitment to their work and their students) and enhanced value-added student outcomes. Researchers found that 'for teachers to be resilient and effective', they needed to have a 'strong and enduring sense of efficacy' and to work in morale-building environments of policy, leadership and collegiality (Day, Sammons, & Stobart, 2007 quoted in; Schleicher, 2016, p. 28).

The foregoing discussion indicates that individual teacher excellence and possession of the qualities and skills outlined in the various checklists can only take you so far. More holistic, multilayered approaches are required. As Gunn and Fisk (2013) argue, in order to meet the requirements of the range of internal and external groups invested in facilitating excellent learning outcomes, a comprehensive 'teaching excellence taxonomy' is needed that seeks develop 'a shared repertoire around teaching and teacher excellence [which] recognises that teaching excellence embraces but is not confined to teacher excellence' (p. 7).

CONCLUSION

Leaving aside the challenges of measuring teaching excellence that have been explored in a voluminous literature (e.g., see Ashwin, 2017; Berger & Wild, 2016; Greatbach & Holland, 2016; O'Leary, 2017; O'Leary & Wood, 2019; Wood & Su, 2017), the difficulties of developing capability and demonstrating quality in teaching should not be underestimated. A number of the sector-wide and institutional schemes, outlined earlier, have sought (directly and indirectly) to raise the standards of teaching in the sector and have clearly had an impact.

However, teaching excellence (as a concept and as a systematic approach) remains a bit of a chimera. Although many claim to recognise it when they see it, there has been relatively little sustained or rigorous research into what teaching excellence looks like or how precisely it impacts on student learning and development. This is borne out in an analysis of

TEF2 submissions (Moore et al., 2017) which indicated something of the richness and diversity of activity, stimulated by or aligned with the notion of teaching excellence, taking place in UK universities, and also revealed 'a lack of systematic evaluation of impact' (HEA, 2017, p. 5). Indeed, 'where evaluation did appear, this tended to relate to specific pedagogic interventions or innovations rather than being institution-wide' (p. 5). 'Deep excellence' – systemic, embedded and almost taken for granted – as articulated in the introductory chapter, appears to be as elusive as the definitions explored there.

This may be because teaching is a complex, multifaced practice; and, as numerous researchers have attested, teaching and learning is contextual, personal and situational and correspondingly difficult to demonstrate or measure accurately (for example, see De Courcy, 2015; Dinetke, Dolmans, Wolfhagen, & Van Der Vleuten, 2004; Fitzmaurice, 2010). This echoes the view of the Warnock Committee in the 'Polytechnic and Colleges' sector 30 years ago, which recognised 'the near impossibility of evaluating teaching quality without seeing the teaching as part of a teaching/learning process, in which the whole process is greater than the sum of its two parts' (Colling, 1989). As Coe (2016) has noted 'learning is invisible', whilst teaching is often described as 'elusive' and 'complex' or even 'mysterious' (Barnett, 2007, p. 115). Furthermore, the connection between student learning and specific teaching practices may at best be tenuous.

In general, although many of the key drivers come from the macro level, teaching excellence in HE is mainly played out at the meso and micro levels. The interactions between these levels are complex and varied and the literature highlights some of the tensions between top-down performative imperatives and bottom-up transformative approaches. A focus on the performative aspects of teaching excellence can stifle risk-taking and lead to an emphasis on compliance rather than excellence. However, as signalled strongly in the literature, it is difficult to achieve teaching excellence in a vacuum without appropriate institutional policies and practices to support it.

Some of the key institutional mechanisms and activities that pertain to teaching excellence feature in literature reviewed above. For example, it is notable that the eminence afforded to teaching excellence in institutional recognition and reward structures has continued to grow, but it is still unevenly distributed and faces challenges as academic roles change. Equally, TEA schemes, though containing many positive features, may encourage a focus on individual 'star' teachers rather than sustainable structures and may tend to valorise one-off innovation over consistency and strength over time. Well-honed, embedded and consistent excellence is often overlooked in the discourse. Some of these weaknesses have been mitigated by the extension and diversification of award schemes, to include team work and collective endeavour. In addition, the growth of the HEA Fellowship scheme (though not explicitly concerned with teaching excellence) has provided opportunities for the recognition of sustained reflective engagement in HE teaching and the development of a supportive community of practice.

The strong connection between institutional or departmental research strengths and excellent teaching is routinely asserted and is highlighted regularly in TEF2 submissions. However, the literature reviewed earlier does not reveal compelling evidence that research excellence and teaching excellence are intrinsically and intimately related, though it indicates that they are likely to have more than a passing acquaintance. Instead, it suggests that a more nuanced approach may be needed in relation to the research-teaching nexus. It should not be automatically assumed that cutting-edge research is a vital and necessary component of teaching excellence, though developing research-like attributes and a culture of enquiry may serve to enhance student outcomes and support a holistic notion of excellence. Students only benefit from a research-rich environment if conscious steps are taken to nurture an active research and learning community.

The disciplinary dimension of teaching excellence is sometimes difficult to tease out as it is often operating in parallel with programme-driven approaches or is overlain with institutional considerations. The prime focus of individual teachers usually lies within departmental and disciplinary structures, and, despite some countervailing pressures, disciplinary signature pedagogies remain important. However, they impact on teaching excellence in complex ways. The literature reviewed generally recognises the centrality of the subject discipline dimension as a key facet of teaching excellence and also acknowledges that it has been little researched and rarely explicated. More work is needed to explore how the identity of a discipline is reflected in the operationalisation of teaching excellence.

Individual teacher excellence remains a constant feature of the literature and everyday discussion of teaching excellence. Much work has been done at different stages of education to try to identify (and almost bottle) the qualities that define an excellent teacher. The resulting checklists have plenty of areas of overlap – particularly emphasising sustained engagement with students and deep subject expertise – and provide useful generic indicators of desirable skills and qualities. In general, however, many would argue that excellent teaching abilities extend beyond an easily describable set of skills and attributes (e.g., Bartram et al., 2019; Su & Wood, 2012). Su and Wood's (2012) account of 'conceptions of teaching' range from 'technical-rational' competency-based approaches to visions 'which emphasise teaching as virtuous practice involving a complex interplay of emotion, "passion" and what we might call a certain indefinable "something"' (p. 143).

The difficulties and dilemmas revealed in this discussion of the challenges of operationalising teaching excellence provide a sobering reality check for the TEF's architects and guardians. As Ashwin (2017) notes,

> *If the TEF ends up being based on measures that are unrelated to the quality of teaching, then the danger is that it will be more about institutional game playing than it is about excellent teaching*

(p. 11)

Yet Ashwin et al. (2012) also point out 'that good teaching is multidimensional and improving it is time-consuming and challenging' (p. 2). Furthermore, the mantra articulated by Baroness Warnock's committee three decades ago remains valid: 'Measuring Quality *does not by itself* ensure improvement' (Colling, 1989). School teachers and FE college lecturers, with their long experience on metric-driven approaches, would recognise firsthand the risks for HE that Berger and Wild (2016) articulate in relation to 'the skewing of behaviours and the homogenization of provision in an effort to excel at specific data gathering exercises' (p. 18).

These concerns about the unintended consequences and possibly distorting impact of the TEF on institutional practices and individual behaviours are echoed in a 2019 survey of HE staff (O'Leary et al., 2019) which reported 'the ratcheting up of monitoring mechanisms and accountability procedures involving both staff and students' (p. 5) including 'a flood of top-down, centralised initiatives, projects and activities introduced to manage and monitor the quality of teaching' (p66). The report also notes that

> *While there was broad acknowledgement … of the need for teaching staff to be accountable for the quality of the programmes they delivered, many [participants] objected to what they perceived as misguided emphasis on measures that seemed to be driven by the requirements of their institution's TEF submission rather than actions that would make a real difference to students' learning or support their needs.*
>
> (p. 68)

Yet, despite the protestations that the framework is 'metric-led not metrics-determined' (Husbands, 2017), and the evidence of the impact of institutions' written 15-page submissions on final ratings (Gillard, 2018; HEA, 2017), the TEF's champions continue to face the dilemma summed up neatly in the reflections of a Senior Army Advisor speaking about the Vietnam War: 'The problem with the War, as it often is, are the metrics. It is a situation where, if you can't count what's important, you make what you can count important' (Burns & Novick, 2017).

The strength and persistence of these concerns have encouraged the development of alternative visions of how teaching excellence might be operationalised in the sector. These go back to earlier more holistic conceptions of teaching excellence underpinned by cooperative principles and sustained by collegial practices (Gibbs, 2008; Skelton, 2007, 2009; Su & Wood, 2012). They highlight the relational, emotional and ethical dimensions of teaching and emphasise the importance of 'academics and students working together to create and develop academic experiences that are authentic, meaningful and transformative to both' (O'Leary & Wood, 2019, p. 15). In this iteration, teaching excellence is 'a collective rather than an individual activity' (O'Leary et al., 2019, p. 4): 'a virtuous and moral enterprise' (Su & Wood, 2012, p. 143) informed by an ethos of professional responsibility rather than an imperative of performative accountability.

REFERENCES

Abbas, A., Brennan, J., Abbas, J., Gantogtokh, O., & Bryman, K. (2016). *Teaching excellence in the disciplines*. York: Higher Education Academy.

Ashwin, P. (2017). What is the Teaching Excellence Framework, and will it work? *International Higher Education*, *88*, 10–11.

Ashwin, P., Abbas, A., & McLean, M. (2012). *Quality and inequality in undergraduate courses: A guide for national and institutional policy makers. Project Report*. Nottingham: University of Nottingham.

Barber, M., & Mourshed, M. (2007). *How the world's best-performing school systems come out on top*. London and Washington, DC: McKinsey.

Barnett, R. (2007). *A will to learn*. Maidenhead: Open University Press.

Bartram, B., Hathaway, T., & Rao, N. (2019). 'Teaching excellence' in higher education: A comparative study of English and Australian academics' perspectives. *Journal of Further and Higher Education*, *43*(9), 1284–1298. doi: 10.1080/0309877X.2018.1479518

Becher, T. (1989). *Academic tribes and territories*. Buckingham: SRHE/Open University Press.

Becher, T., & Trowler, P. R. (2001). *Academic tribes and territories: Intellectual enquiry and the culture of disciplines*. Buckingham: SRHE / Open University Press.

Berger, D., & Wild, C. (2016). The Teaching Excellence Framework: Would you tell me, please, which way we ought to go from here? *Higher Education Review*, *48*(3), 5–22.

Bergseth, B., Petocz, P., & Abrandt Dahlgren, M. (2014). Ranking quality in higher education: Guiding or misleading? *Quality in Higher Education*, *20*(3), 330–347.

Blackmore, P. (2009). Conceptions of academic development in higher education institutions. *Studies in Higher Education*, *34*(6), 663–679.

Botterill, D. (2013). *Reports of the 2010 national teaching fellows: A synthesis*. York: Higher Education Academy.

Brabon, B. (2016, May 19). Beyond the Rubicon: Exploring the TEF in the disciplines [HEA blog post]. Retrieved from https://www.heacademy.ac.uk/blog/beyond-rubicon-exploring-tef-disciplines-dr-ben-brabon-hea

Bradley, S., Kirby, E., & Madriaga, M. (2015). What students value as inspirational and transformative teaching. *Innovations in Education & Teaching International*, *52*(3), 231–242.

Brew, A. (2007). Integrating research and teaching: Understanding excellence. In A. Skelton (Ed.) *International perspectives on teaching excellence in higher education: Improving knowledge and practice* (pp. 74–88). Abingdon: Routledge.

Brockerhoff, L., Stensaker, B., & Huisman, J. (2014). Prescriptions and perceptions of teaching excellence: A study of the national 'Wettbewerb Exzellente Lehre' initiative in Germany. *Quality in Higher Education*, *20*(3), 235–254.

Brusoni, M., Damian, R., Sauri, J. G., Jackson, S., Komurcugil, H., Malmedy, M., … Zobel, L. (2014). *The concept of excellence in higher education*. Brussels: European Association for Quality Assurance in Higher Education (ENQA). Retrieved from http://www.enqa.eu/index.php/publications/papers-reports/occasional-papers/

Bryson, C. (Ed.). (2014). *Understanding and developing student engagement: Perspectives from universities and students*. Abingdon: Routledge.

Burke, P. J., & Crozier, G. (2012). *Teaching inclusively: Challenging pedagogical spaces*. York: Higher Education Academy.

Burns, K. & Novick, L. (2017). *The Vietnam war. [Interview with James Willbanks, Episode 3]*. Arlington, VA: PBS Distribution.

Cashmore, A., Cane, C., & Cane, R. (2013). *Rebalancing promotion in the HE sector: Is teaching excellence being rewarded?* York: Higher Education Academy. Retrieved from https://www.heacademy.ac.uk/system/files/hea_reward_publication_rebalancingpromotion_0.pdf

Chick, N. L., Haynie, A., & Guring, R. A. R. (2009). From generic to signature pedagogies. In R. A. R. Gurung, N. L. Chick, & A. Haynie (Eds.), *Exploring signature pedagogies: Approaches to teaching disciplinary habits of mind*. Sterling, VA: Stylus.

Cleaver, E., Lintern, M., & McLinden, M. (2014). *Teaching and learning in higher education: Disciplinary approaches to educational enquiry*. London: SAGE Publications.

Coe, R. (2016, July 6). What makes great teaching? SSAT and the Prince's teaching Institute conference. Keynote presentation. Retrieved from: https://webcontent.ssatuk.co.uk/

wp-content/uploads/2016/07/08132401/What-makes-great-teaching-Rob-Coe-1.pdf

Coe, R., Aloisi, C., Higgins, S., & Major, L. E. (2014). *What makes great teaching? Review of the underpinning research*. Durham: Sutton Trust/University of Durham.

Colley, H., & Healey, M. (2012). *Analysis of the learning and teaching strategies 2011/12 to 2013/14 in Wales*. York: Higher Education Academy.

Colling, C. (1989). In Pursuit of quality: Summary of points arising from committee papers, July 5th 1989. PCFC Committee of Inquiry into teaching quality. London: Polytechnics and Colleges Funding Council.

Davies, R., Hope, M., & Robertson, A. (2012). *Student-led teaching awards*. York: Higher Education Academy.

Daw, P., & Robinson, C. (2013). *To the next level: Improving secondary school teaching to outstanding*. Reading: CfBT Education Trust.

Day, C., Sammons, P., & Stobart, G. (2007). *Teachers matter: Connecting work, lives and effectiveness*. Maidenhead: McGraw-Hill.

De Courcy, E. (2015). Defining and measuring teaching excellence in higher education in the 21st century. *The College Quarterly*, *18*(1), 1–6.

Devlin, M., & Samarawickrema, G. (2010). The criteria of effective teaching in a changing higher education context. *Higher Education Research and Development, 29*(2), 111–124.

Dinetke, T., Dolmans, D., Wolfhagen, I., & Van Der Vleuten, C. (2004). The development and validation of a framework for teaching competencies in higher education. *Higher Education*, *48*(2), 253–268.

D'Andrea, V. (2007). National strategies for promoting excellence in teaching: A critical review. In: A. Skelton (Ed.), *International perspectives on teaching excellence in higher education: Improving knowledge and practice* (pp. 169–182). Abingdon: Routledge.

D'Andrea, V., & Gosling, D. (2005). *Improving teaching and learning in higher education: A whole institution approach*. Maidenhead: Open University Press/McGraw Hill.

Entwistle, N. (2009). *Teaching for understanding at university: Deep approaches and distinctive ways of thinking*. London: Palgrave Macmillan.

Evans, C. (2000). Against excellence. *Educational Developments*, *1*(2), 7.

Fanghanel, J. (2007). Teaching excellence in context: Drawing from a socio-cultural approach. In A. Skelton (Ed.), *International perspectives on teaching excellence in higher education: Improving knowledge and practice* (pp. 197–212) Abingdon: Routledge.

Fanghanel, J., Pritchard, J., Potter, J., & Wisker, G. (2015). *Defining and supporting the scholarship of teaching and learning (SoTL): A sector-wide study*. York: Higher Education Academy.

Fitzmaurice, M. (2010). Considering teaching in higher education as a practice. *Teaching in Higher Education*, *15*(1), 45–55.

Foster, E., & Southwell-Sander, J. (2014). The NTSU outstanding teaching awards: Student perspectives on engagement. In C. Bryson (Ed.), *Understanding and developing student engagement* (pp. 139–150). London: Routledge.

Gale, R. A. (2007). Braided practice: The place of scholarly enquiry in teaching excellence. In A. Skelton (Ed.), *International perspectives on teaching excellence in higher education: Improving knowledge and practice*. Abingdon: Routledge.

Gibbs, G. (2007). Have we lost the plot with teaching awards? *Academy Exchange*, 7, 40–42.

Gibbs, G. (2008). *Conceptions of teaching excellence underlying teaching award schemes*. York: Higher Education Academy.

Gibbs, G. (2012). *Implications of 'dimensions of quality' in a market environment*. HEA Research Series. York: Higher Education Academy.

Gibbs, G., & Habeshaw, T. (2002). *Recognising and rewarding excellent teaching: A guide to good practice*. Milton Keynes: Open University Press.

Gillard, J. W. (2018). An initial analysis and reflection of the metrics used in the Teaching Excellence Framework in the UK. *Perspectives: Policy and Practice in Higher Education*, 22(2), 49–57. doi:10.1080/13603108.2017.1409669

Graham, R. (2015). *Does teaching advance your academic career? Perspectives of promotion procedures in UK higher education*. London: Royal Academy of Engineering.

Graham, R. (2016). *Does teaching advance your academic career? Interim report on the development of a template for evaluation teaching achievement*. London: Royal Academy of Engineering.

Greatbatch, D., & Holland, J. (2016). *Teaching quality in higher education: Literature review and qualitative research*. London: BIS.

Gunn, V. (2013). Mimetic desire and intersubjectivity in disciplinary cultures: Constraints or enablers to learning in higher education? *Studies in Continuing Education*, 36(1), 67–82. doi:10.1080/0158037X.787981

Gunn, V., & Fisk, A. (2013). *Considering teaching excellence in higher education: 2007–2013. A literature review since the CHERI report 2007*. York: Higher Education Academy.

Hammer, D., Piascik, P., Medina, M., Pittenger, A., Rose, R., Creekmore, F., … Steven, S. (2010). Recognition of teaching excellence. *American Journal of Pharmaceutical Education*, 74, 1–11.

Hanushek, E. (2010). The difference is great teachers. In Webber, K., (Ed.) *Waiting for 'Superman': How we can save America's failing public schools (pp. 81–100)*, New York, NY: Public Affairs.

Hattie, J., & Marsh, H. (1996). The relationship between research and teaching: A meta-analysis. *Review of Educational Research*, 66, 507–542.

Hay, D., Weller, S., & Ashton, K. (2015). Researcher-led teaching: Embodiment of academic practice. *Higher Education Review*, 48(1), 25–39.

HEA (Higher Education Academy). (2005). *Higher education Academy commentary on: Welsh institutional learning and teaching strategies 2004–05*. York: Higher Education Academy.

HEA (Higher Education Academy). (2016, May 12). Call for the National Teaching Fellowship Scheme 2016 includes a new collaborative team award [Press release]. Retrieved from https://www.heacademy.ac.uk/about/news/call-national-teaching-fellowship-scheme-2016-includes-new-collaborative-team-award

HEA (Higher Education Academy). (2017). *HEA reflections on 'Evidencing teaching excellence'*. York: Higher Education Academy.

Healey, M., & Jenkins, A. (2009). *Developing undergraduate research and inquiry*. York: Higher Education Academy.

Henard, F., & Roseveare, D. (2012). *Fostering quality teaching in higher education: Policies and practices*. Paris: OECD Publishing.

Husbands, C. (2017, June 23). Universities, don't rest on your laurels - use the TEF to improve. *The Guardian*. Retrieved from https://www.theguardian.com/higher-education-network/2017/jun/23/universities-tef-improve.

Jenkins, A., & Healey, M. (2007). Critiquing excellence: Undergraduate research for all students. In A. Skelton (Ed.), *International perspectives on teaching excellence in higher education: Improving knowledge and practice* (pp. 117–132). Abingdon: Routledge.

Jenkins, A., Healey, M., & Zetter, R. (2007). *Linking teaching and research in disciplines and departments*. York: Higher Education Academy.

Jones, J., & Wisker, G., (2012). Educational development in the UK. Report for the Heads of Educational Development Group (HEDG). University of Brighton, Brighton. Retrieved from: http://www.hedg.ac.uk/ico/wp-content/uploads/2016/02/HEDGFinalReport2012.pdf

Kreber, C. (Ed.). (2009). *The university and its disciplines: Teaching and learning within and beyond disciplinary boundaries.* London: Routledge.

Land, R., & Gordon, G. (2015). *Teaching excellence initiatives: Modalities and operational factors.* York: Higher Education Academy.

Layton, C., & Brown, C. (2011). Striking a balance: Supporting teaching excellence award applications. *International Journal for Academic Development*, *16*(2), 163–174.

Leibowitz, B., van Schalkwyk, S., Ruiters, J., Farmer, J., & Adendorff, H. (2012). 'It's been a wonderful life': Accounts of the interplay between structure and agency by 'good' university teachers. *Higher Education*, *63*, 353–365.

Little, B., Locke, W., Parker, J., & Richardson, J. (2007). *Excellence in teaching and learning: A review of the literature for the higher education Academy.* York: Higher Education Academy.

Lubicz-Nawrocka, T., & Bunting, K. (2019). Student perceptions of teaching excellence: An analysis of student-led teaching award nomination data. *Teaching in Higher Education*, *24*(1), 63–80. doi:10.1080/13562517.2018.1461620

Macfarlane, B. (2007). Beyond performance in teaching excellence. In A. Skelton (Ed.), *International perspectives on teaching excellence in higher education: Improving knowledge and practice* (pp. 48–59) Abingdon: Routledge.

Macfarlane, B. (2011). Prizes, pedagogic research and teaching professors: Lowering the status of teaching and learning through bifurcation. *Teaching in Higher Education*, *16*, 127–130.

Madriaga, M., & Morley, K. (2016). Awarding teaching excellence: 'what is it supposed to achieve?' teacher perceptions of student-led awards. *Teaching in Higher Education*, *21*(2), 166–174. doi:10.1080/13562517.2015.1136277

McAleavy, T. (2013, May 2). The five ingredients of outstanding teaching. [blog post] SecEd. Retrieved from: http://www.sec-ed.co.uk/best-practice/the-five-ingredients-of-outstanding-teaching

McCulloch, A. (2009). The student as co-producer: Learning from public administration about the student-university relationship. *Studies in Higher Education*, *34*(2), 171–183.

McKnight, K., Graybeal, L., Yarbro, J., & Graybeal, J. (2016). *England: What makes an effective teacher?*. London: Pearson.

Moore, J., Higham, L., Sanders, J., Jones, S., Candarli, D., & Mountford-Zimdars, A. (2017). *Evidencing teaching excellence: Analysis of the teaching excellence framework (TEF2) provider submissions*. York: Higher Education Academy.

Mountford-Zimdars, A., Sabri, D., Moore, J., Sanders, J., Jones, S., & Higham, L. (2015). *Causes of differences in student outcomes*. Bristol: Higher Education Funding Council for England.

Murphy, J., Griffen, C. & Higgs, B. (Eds.). (2010). Research-Teaching linkages: Practice and policy. In *Proceedings of the Irish national Academy for integration of research, teaching and learning, 3rd annual conference*, NAIRTL, Cork.

National Committee of Inquiry into Higher Education (NCIHE). (1997). Higher education for a learning society. Dearing Report. HMSO, London.

National Forum for the Enhancement of Teaching and Learning in Higher Education (2016). *What does it take to be a teaching hero? Exploring students' perceptions and experiences of impactful, transformative teaching in Irish higher education.* Dublin: National Forum.

Neary, M. (2016). Teaching excellence framework: A critical response and an alternative future. *Journal of Contemporary European Research*, *12*(3), 690–695.

Olsson, T., & Roxå, T. (2013). Assessing and rewarding excellent academic teachers for the benefit of an organisation. *European Journal of Higher Education*, *3*(1), 40–61.

O'Leary, M. (2017). Monitoring and measuring teaching excellence in higher education: From contrived competition to collective collaboration. In: A. French, & M. O'Leary (Eds.), *Teaching excellence in higher education: Challenges, changes and the teaching excellence framework* (pp. 5–38). Bingley: Emerald Publishing.

O'Leary, M., Cui, V., & French, A. (2019). *Understanding, recognising and rewarding teaching quality in higher education: An exploration of the impact and implications of the Teaching Excellence Framework – A project report for UCU.* London: Universities and Colleges Union. Retrieved from http://www.ucu.org.uk/media/10092/Impact-of-TEF-report-Feb-2019/pdf/ImpactofTEFreportFEb2019.

O'Leary, M., & Wood, P. (2019). Reimagining teaching excellence: Why collaboration, rather than competition, holds the key to improving teaching and learning in higher education. *Educational Review*,*71*(1), 122–139. doi: 10.1080/00131911.2019.1524203

Parpala, A., Lindblom-Ylänne, S., & Rytkönen, H. (2011). Students' conceptions of good teaching in three different disciplines. *Assessment & Evaluation in Higher Education,* *36*(5), 549–563.

Potter, J. (2008). Starting with the discipline. In R. Murray (Ed.), *The scholarship of teaching and learning in higher education* (pp. 58–68). Maidenhead: SRHE/Open University Press.

QAA (Quality Assurance Agency). (2015). *Higher education review: Second year findings 2014–2015.* Gloucester: QAA.

QAA (Quality Assurance Agency) Scotland (2008). Sector-wide discussions: Vol 2 - vignettes of practice. QAA Scotland, Glasgow. Retrieved from https://www.enhancementthemes. ac.uk/completed-enhancement-themes/research-teaching-linkages

Revell, A., & Wainwright, E. (2009). What makes lectures 'unmissable'? Insights into teaching excellence and active learning. *Journal of Geography in Higher Education,* *33*(2), 209–223.

Rickinson, M., Spencer, R., & Stainton, C. (2012). *NTFS review 2012: Report on findings.* York: Higher Education Academy.

Robinson, W., & Hilli, A. (2016). The English 'Teaching Excellence Framework' and professionalising teaching and learning in research-intensive universities: An exploration of opportunities, challenges, rewards and values from a recent empirical study. *Foro de Educación,* *14*(21), 151–165.

Robson, S., Wall, K., & Lofthouse, R. (2013). Raising the profile of innovative teaching in higher education? Reflections on the EquATE project. *International Journal of Teaching and Learning in Higher Education, 25*(1), 92–102.

Roxå, T., Olsson, T., & Mårtensson, K. (2008). Appropriate use of theory in the scholarship of teaching and learning as a strategy for institutional development. *Arts and Humanities in Higher Education, 7*(3), 276–294.

Sammons, P., Kington, A., Lindorff-Vijayendran, A., & Ortega, L. (2016). *Inspiring teachers: Perspectives and practices.* Reading: Education Development Trust.

Sanders, J. (2010). Horray for Harvard? The fetish of footnotes revisited. *Journal of Widening Participation and Lifelong Learning, 12,* 48–59.

Schleicher, A. (2016). *Teaching excellence through professional learning and policy reform: Lessons from around the world. International summit on the teaching profession.* Paris: OECD Publishing.

Shephard, K., Harland, T., Stein, S., & Tidswell, T. (2011). Preparing an application for a higher-education teaching-excellence award: Whose foot fits Cinderella's shoe? *Journal of Higher Education Policy and Management, 33*(1), 47–56.

Skelton, A. (2004). Understanding 'teaching excellence' in higher education: A critical evaluation of the national teaching fellowships scheme. *Studies in Higher Education, 29*(4), 451–468.

Skelton, A. (2005). *Understanding teaching excellence in higher education: Towards a critical approach.* London: Routledge.

Skelton, A. (Ed.), (2007). *International perspectives on teaching excellence in higher education: Improving knowledge and practice.* Abingdon: Routledge.

Skelton, A. (2009.) A 'teaching excellence' for the times we live in? *Teaching in Higher Education, 14*(1), 107–112.

van der Sluis, H., Burden, P., & Huet, I. (2017). Retrospection and reflection: The emerging influence of an institutional professional recognition scheme on professional development and academic practice in a UK university. *Innovations in Education & Teaching International, 54*(2), 126–134. doi:10.1080/14703297.2016.1273790

Su, F., & Wood, M. (2012). What makes a good university lecturer? Students' perceptions of teaching excellence. *Journal of Applied Research in Higher Education, 4*(2), 142–155.

Thompson, C. A., & Wolstencroft, P. (2014). 'Give 'em the old razzle dazzle' – surviving the lesson observation process in further education. *Research in Post-Compulsory Education, 19*(3), 261–275.

Thompson, S. & Zeitzeva, E. (2012.) *Reward and recognition: Student-led teaching awards report.* York: Higher Education Academy.

Trowler, P., & Wareham, T. (2007). *Tribes, territories, research and teaching: Enhancing the 'teaching-research nexus'.* York: Higher Education Academy.

Turner, R., & Gosling, D. (2012). Rewarding excellent teaching: The translation of a policy initiative in the United Kingdom. *Higher Education Quarterly, 66*(4), 415–430.

Turner, N., Oliver, M., McKenna, C., Hughes, J., Smith, H., Deepwell, F., & Strives, L. (2013). *Measuring the impact of the UK Professional Standards Framework for teaching & supporting learning (UKPSF).* York: The Higher Education Academy.

Välimaa, J. & O.-H. Ylijoki, (Eds.). (2010). *Cultural perspectives on higher education*. Dordrecht: Springer.

Wood, M., & Su, F. (2017). What makes an excellent lecturer? Academics' perspectives on the discourse of 'teaching excellence' in higher education. *Teaching in Higher Education*, 22(4), 451–466.

Yarkova, T., & Cherp, A. (2013). Managing the sacred? Perspectives on teaching excellence and learning outcomes from an international postgraduate university. *European Journal of Higher Education*, 3(1), 24–39. doi:10.1080/21568235.2013.778047

Young, P. (2006). Out of balance: Lecturers' perceptions of differential status and rewards in relation to teaching and research. *Teaching in Higher Education*, 11, 191–202.

3

'WISHING WON'T MAKE IT SO': DELIVEROLOGY, TEF AND THE WICKED PROBLEM OF INCLUSIVE TEACHING EXCELLENCE

Julian Crockford

ABSTRACT

The Teaching Excellence Framework was explicitly introduced as a mechanism to 'enhance teaching' in universities. This chapter suggests, however, that the highly complex 'black box' methodology used to calculate TEF outcomes effectively blunts its purpose as a policy lever. As a result, TEF appears to function primarily as performative policy act, merely gesturing towards a concern with social mobility. Informed by the data and metrics driven Deliverology approach to public management, I suggest the opacity of the TEF's assessment approach enables policymakers to distance themselves from and sidestep the wicked problems raised by the complicated contexts of contemporary higher education learning and teaching. At the same time, however, I argue that the very indeterminacy through which the framework achieves this sleight of hand creates a space in which engaged teaching practitioners can push through a more progressive approach to inclusive success.

Keywords: Teaching excellence framework; TEF assessment methodology; policy formation; policy levers; wicked problems; inclusive learning and teaching; deliverology

We will enhance teaching in our universities by implementing the Teaching Excellence Framework (TEF), using a phased approach.

–DBIS (2016)

'Wishing won't make it so' is a 1958 Everly Brothers song of personal defeat, or a thumbnail of Ayn Rand's Objectivist philosophy (Rand, 1989). Irrespective of one's preferred frame of cultural reference, however, the implication is the same; outcomes do not automatically flow from the desire for them. This logic, which disconnects outcomes from intention, applies also, I suggest, to the intended function of the UK's Teaching Excellence Framework (TEF) as a policy lever for shifting higher education's learning and teaching practice into an increasingly inclusive domain.

The TEF emerges as a by-product of the ongoing deformation of the UK HE sector by broader structural pressures, not least the brute force application of a neoliberal free market logic. In the pages below, I suggest that the TEF is a condensed configuration of these tensions, generated by policymakers as they attempt to simultaneously shift the costs of HE onto students themselves and transform the sector into a competitive market, whilst still appearing to promote fair access and social mobility.

Part of the issue is that the teaching excellence and inclusivity challenges articulated, albeit loosely and selectively, by TEF metrics already constitute wicked problems (Bore & Wright, 2009) for the HE sector, throwing up a range of highly complex, context-dependent issues for which no macro-level solutions currently exist. As such, the TEF begins to look like a largely performative policy act, through which policymakers can 'perform' a concern with HE inclusion and social mobility, without having to engage directly with the highly complex challenges it throws up. Considered in this way, policymakers' gestures towards issues of social justice begin to look increasingly hollow, a fig leaf to spare the blushes of those nakedly ambitious for the English higher education system to become a full consumer market.

Nonetheless, I end with a note of optimism, by suggesting that the very 'wickedity' lying at the heart of the TEF could also create space for learning and teaching practitioners to engage in what Ball (1993; 2015) describes as policy 'ad hockery'; the exploitation of gaps and loopholes in the logic of a policy text to turn it to alternative ends; in this case, the creation of space within individual HEIs to research, test and develop ways of making so a collective wish for inclusive learning and teaching.

EMERGENCE

Neoliberalism has emerged as a key metanarrative in recent years, through which the contemporary transformation of higher education is increasingly understood. But as Ball (2012) observes, it is also 'one of those terms which is so widely and loosely used that it is in danger of becoming a detached signifier' (p. 18). For some commentators,

neoliberalism was born out of intensified globalisation in the
1970s (Giroux, 2014; Morrison, Cannella, & Koro-Ljungberg,
2017) or the frenzy of market deregulation in the 1980s
(Bessant, Robinson, & Ormerod, 2015; Harvey, 2007; Pusser
& Marginson, 2013). Most agree that it can be characterised
by increasing state intervention to develop markets in public
arenas (Olssen & Peters, 2005; Savigny, 2013); increasing
emphasis on entrepreneurialism and free trade (Ball, 2012;
Harvey, 2007); the application of market logic to new areas,
such as public services, with clients being transformed, often
unwittingly or unwillingly, into consumers, and the rise of a
new species of (micro-)manager brandishing performative
technologies (Blackmore, 2009; Holloway & Brass, 2018;
Woodall, Hiller, & Resnick, 2014; Zepke, 2018).

Managerialism and performativity, in particular, are also
associated with the rise of New Public Management (NPM)
(Johnsen, 2005; Marginson, 2013; Sarrico, Rosa, Teixeira,
& Cardoso, 2010). For Hood (1995), this policy approach
emerged during the 1980s on the back of high levels of trust
in marketisation and privatisation logics and low levels of
trust in public servants and their professionalism. Implicit in
the latter was an assumption that the state and the public
purse needed to be protected from its own custodians. For
New Public Managers, the solution was to carefully monitor
and measure outputs of the public services under their
stewardship, usually by imposing a panoptic regime of
reifying and reductive performance indicators. As Steer et al.
(2007) put it,

> ...national governments have withdrawn from direct
> control over the administration of public services [...
> and] policy levers, such as performance targets,
> standards, audit, inspection, quality assurance
> processes and powers to intervene where public

> *services are 'failing', have consequently become*
> *central instruments in a system of arms-length*
> *regulation.*

(pp. 176, 177)

For the HE sector specifically, neoliberalism presents as a syndrome consisting of many symptoms; policy changes at the global level (Ball, 2016; Blackmore, 2009; Marginson 2011, 2013), the injection of marketisation, privatisation and corporate logics (Ball, 2012; Giroux, 2014; Mahony & Weiner, 2019; Olssen & Peters, 2005); and an increasing focus on fabricating intra-sector competition (Blackmore, 2009; Ingleby, 2015; Sabri, 2011). As a result, students have been repositioned as consumers and customers (Bovill et al 2016; Hall, 2013; Ingleby, 2015; Marginson, 2013; Nixon, Scullion, & Hearn, 2018; Woodall et al. 2014), in turn generating a need for HE providers to demonstrate the return on their substantial financial investment (Forstenzer, 2016; Jones, 2013; Marginson, 2006), which is often crudely tallied in terms of their potential postgraduation earnings (Ingleby, 2015; Morrison et al. 2017; Polkinghorne, Roushan, & Taylor, 2017). As such, neoliberalism tosses more ingredients into the traditional stew of policy tensions that simmer between the challenge of funding the HE system and deciding who should benefit from it, issues that have seasoned political concern with higher education, since at least the 1963 publication of the Robbins report (McCaig 2016, 2019; Savigny, 2013; Trow, 1973).

'WE CARE' – TARGET SETTING AND SOCIAL MOBILITY

Despite these broader structural transformations, however, political convention and public expectation also require the

Government and policymakers to attend to social and moral issues (Ball, 2012; Hockings, 2010; Marginson, 2011). As Bowl (2019) suggests, when addressing HE, 'it would be deemed unacceptable for a government not to profess some kind of commitment to equality, equity, fairness or social mobility' (p. 12). In the same vein, Green and Kynaston (2019) suggest, 'rather like corporate social responsibility in the business world, social mobility has become one of those motherhood-and-apple-pie causes that it is almost rude not to utter warm words about'.

From this perspective, the TEF begins to look like an ideological masterstroke that makes it possible to both have and eat the marketisation cake. The framework was originally devised to generate market data for the rational *student economicus* conjured by the 2016 HE White Paper; 'information, particularly on price and quality, is critical if the higher education market is to perform properly' (DBIS 2016, p. 11). But at the same time, it was positioned as a policy lever to drive up the quality of HE teaching for 'all students' including 'those from disadvantaged backgrounds' (DBIS 2016, p. 14). As I will discuss below, however, the net result is that responsibility for ensuring equality and social justice is quickly deferred downwards onto HE providers themselves, thereby enabling policymakers to distance and insulate themselves from the highly complex challenges their own policies raise. In delegating responsibility for devising and implementing practical solutions downwards, the TEF owes much to the 'Deliverology' approach to Public Management.

Deliverology sprang forth as a localised expression of NPM, during New Labour's tenure in Government, via the formation of The Prime Minister's Delivery Unit (PMDU) (Ball, Maguire, Braun, Perryman, & Hoskins, 2012; Riddell, 2013). The unit's innovation was to divide performative governance into four key stages: clarifying the social problem;

identifying key stakeholders ('delivery chains'); monitoring progress against sets of carefully chosen metrics, which functioned as 'proxies' for the desired outcomes (Riddell, 2013); and which operated as triggers to action further responses when insufficient progress was being made (Barber, 2011; Nordstrum, LeMahieu, & Dodd, 2017; Ridell 2013).

Formulated in this way, Deliverology operates as a soft power policy lever. For Riddell (2013) such approaches imply

> ...a view of a 'network' or delivery system, but without an assumption of direct leverage. Its role is there to invite (but not pressurise) a variety of independent, Governmental and private sector organisations to participate in the process of change, as integral partners, not just as consultees.

> (p. 855)

Ball (2012) and Ball et al. (2012), however, suggest that the imposition of such performative mechanisms onto the compulsory education sector is much less benign that this reading implies. Instead, they argue, it serves to impose a Foucaultian performative 'discipline' or 'technology' on the 'souls' of teachers, driving their professional practices, identities and even their 'selves', as well as those of their students (Ball et al. 2012, p. 523).

Either way, this distribution of responsibilities in Deliverology makes policymakers responsible for articulating the problem, setting the agenda and devising and imposing relevant targets, and the delivery stakeholders further down the chain responsible, with varying degrees of explicitness, for knowing how to resolve these problems and deliver the required solutions. And herein lies Deliverology's Achilles heel, its lack of direct engagement with the problem-solving process, which is exposed when it attempts to engage with areas of complex social reality, such as education. As Nordstrum et al. (2017) put it, at 'one level, Deliverology assumes that solutions are already known. That is, the essential challenge lies in the implementation of solutions' (p. 51). In this reading, while solutions have an explicit role in this process, albeit delegated down 'delivery chains' (Riddell, 2013), from a policymaking perspective they are subordinate to the real business of measuring the effectiveness of their implementation (Nordstrum et al. 2017, p. 48).

TEF: A MUTANT DELIVEROLOGY?

First appearing in the Conservative Party Manifesto in 2015, the TEF preceded both the Office for Students and the selection of former PMDU head and chief architect of Deliverology, Michael Barber, as its Director. If the design of the TEF was informed by Deliverology's performative components, it also represented a significant departure. For, as the TEF is configured in the HE White Paper and subsequent regulatory guidance, the deferred positioning of solutions and mechanisms at the base of delivery chains typical of Deliverology elsewhere, is ignored. This omission, the mechanisms and solutions by which targets are to be achieved, is crucial and serves to intensify an already direct relationship between policy-formation and target-setting at the expense of practical delivery considerations in ways that I will discuss below.

The complexity and indeterminacy inherent in the TEF appears at two different levels; the first is structural, a consequence of the complicated design of an assessment methodology that relies on the amalgamation of a range of different metrics, while the second resides in the construction of the metrics themselves.

Structural Complexity

Complexity is a by-product of the TEF's underlying multi-stage assessment approach. The TEF comprises a set of metrics, designed to measure, compare and differentiate the teaching quality of different HE providers (DfE, 2017, p. 8). With the declared pragmatic aim of reducing the regulatory burden on individual providers (DfE, 2017, p. 9), the TEF was designed to draw on existing sector datasets. As such, its architects settled on 6 core metrics (2 each in 'teaching quality', 'learning environment' and 'student outcomes and learning gain'). Each of these 6 core metrics draw on established regulatory data; 3 from National Student Survey (NSS) outcomes data, 1 from HESA continuation data performance indicators and 2 from the Destinations of Leavers of Higher Education (DLHE) survey outcomes. They are bolstered by supplementary metrics and a provider-supplied explanatory narrative.

Policy concerns with social justice, mobility and widening participation issues are articulated in the framework, via 'split metrics'. Each of the 6 core measures are sub-divided into separate metrics based on pre-existing policy definitions of disadvantage and under-representation (young and mature students, sex, the POLAR indicator of local HE participation rates, region-specific Index of Multiple Disadvantage (IMD) rankings, disability, ethnicity and domicile), many of which are further reduced to binary categories.

The assessment of an HE provider's teaching excellence as described in the 2017 *Teaching Excellence and Student Outcomes Framework Specification* (DfE, 2017) is ultimately expressed through the award of gold, silver or bronze status. These awards represent the outcome of a chain of assessment stages, which in turn rest on a mix of quantitative performance measures and the expert judgement of an assessment panel.

A number of commentators have suggested that the 'supplementary' components considered in the final stage can have a substantial effect on outcomes (Gillard, 2018; Moore, Higham, & Sanders, 2018). As such, and despite its apparent reliance on quantitative data, the 'holistic' TEF assessment process becomes a complex seesaw, relying as much on the panel's subjective weighting and balancing of the different indicators and qualitative data, as on quantitative data. Indeed, the guidance itself notes that assessors must 'make a judgement about the best fit based on the combination of evidence contained in the metrics and submission' (DfE, 2017, p. 66). This reliance on panel judgement transforms what is initially constructed as a data-driven exercise into a 'black box' in which the judgement of the panel and individual assessors, underpinning three of the four assessment stages, takes place (see Table 3.1).

Metric Complexity

The second level of complexity is generated by the design of the TEF metrics themselves and what they purport to measure. We lack space in the current chapter to unpick each of these metrics in detail, but commentary elsewhere provides an efficient dissection of the implications, contradictions and limitations of the various TEF metrics (see, for example, Baker, 2018; Gunn, 2018; Gillard 2018; Tomlinson, Enders, & Naidoo, 2018; Frankham, 2017; Barkas, Scott, Poppitt, & Smith, 2019; Forstenzer, 2016; Canning, 2019 for wide-ranging and satisfying analyses).

Table 3.1. The Stages of the TEF Assessment Process.

Stage	Criteria	Judgement	Guidance Notes (DfE, 2017)
First assessment	Flags generated for 6 core metrics relative to sector-adjusted benchmark/and to indicate top or bottom in sector	Quantitative	The guidance suggests that a preliminary positive score of 2.5 across the 6 core areas should result in an initial hypothesised Gold ranking, an overall negative score of 1.5 or less as Bronze, with providers in between receiving a Silver recommendation (DfE, 2017, p. 6).
Initial hypothesis	Balance of performance in 6 core metrics to decide initial hypothesis and level of confidence in that judgement	Panel judgement	

Table 3.1. (Continued)

Stage	Criteria	Judgement	Guidance Notes (DfE, 2017)
Test initial hypothesis against split metrics	Test initial hypothesis against provider performance in split metrics for each core metric. Panel to consider distribution patterns across all metrics. Panel to consider the significance ranking of metrics causing concern.	Panel judgement	How the relationship between split and core metrics is to be articulated is not explicit in guidance; 'performance with respect to certain student groups, particularly those from disadvantaged backgrounds, must be taken into account in determining a provider's rating' (DfE, 2017, p. 58). Moreover, the panel are to consider the significance of any metric causing concern and its impact on their confidence in their hypothesised ranking.
Consideration of supplementary documents	Supplementary contextual metrics – providing overview of HEI Provider narrative	Panel judgement	

Source: Created by author.

A brief survey of just one aspect of the TEF can serve as an illustration of the complexity inherent in each of the individual metrics. The core metric for 'teaching quality', for example, is defined as a student satisfaction measure of 'the teaching on my course'. It aggregates levels of student agreement with NSS questions 1–4:

- Staff are good at explaining things

- Staff have made the subject interesting

- The course is intellectually stimulating

- My course has challenged me to achieve my best work

  (The Student Survey.com, 2018)

Each student responds to these questions on a 5-point Likert scale of agreement. Responses are collated, compared to an institution specific benchmark and converted into positive and negative rankings, before being split down into student diversity and disadvantage characteristics.

The methodologies and design of the National Student Survey questions are themselves subject to a range of methodological critiques (Bell & Brooks, 2018; Bennett & Kane, 2014; Cocksedge & Taylor, 2013; Canning, 2019; Sabri, 2013; Yorke, 2009). For present purposes, however, it is sufficient to note that the survey, given to students in their final year of study, effectively asks them to sum up what might be three or more years of potentially variable experiences (Parker & Mathews, 2001). As such, it requires respondents to aggregate what might be highly varied and diverse experiences across a range of different modules, teaching contexts, experiences and academic years. Such retrospective questions are also open to recall bias, the tendency to focus on more recent experiences. Moreover, this particular TEF metric is, itself, an aggregation of responses to four separate aspects of the student academic experience. Consequently, it is not possible to relate the metric measure, or its relationship to the benchmark, whether positive or negative, to any specific context. This level of abstraction means that HE providers are effectively unable to devise and position any practical levers or mechanisms through which they can improve specific HE learning and teaching experiences in order to encourage a greater ratio of positive student responses.

Of course, the argument could be made that, as a policy lever, the purpose of the TEF is not to prompt specific responses, but to encourage HE providers to adopt a more holistic approach to inclusive learning and teaching. This argument is weakened, however, by the inclusion of the split metrics, which explicitly encourages exactly this kind of student cohort approach. Nonetheless, even broken down into cohort groupings, the metrics still fail to provide any purchase or reliable steer for HE providers wishing to nudge their next set of metrics in a positive direction.

There is a substantial body of excellent research exploring inclusive learning and teaching in HE. Much of this, however, remains at an exploratory or stall-setting level, or, alternatively, focuses on very specific disciplinary or student cohort contexts. While there is insufficient space here to address this work, several writers have developed relevant literature syntheses; assessment of teaching quality (Greatbatch & Holland, 2016); teaching excellence (Gunn & Fisk, 2013); degree outcome differences (Mountford Zimdars et al. 2015); and inclusive learning and teaching (Hockings, 2010). Even a cursory reading of these summaries provides a clear indication of the large range of factors hypothesised to impact on an individual student's academic experience of HE. Hockings (2010) and Cousin and Cureton (2012), for example, propose a four-part interlocking typology of learning and teaching domains; curriculum and learning, relationships between staff and students, social, cultural and economic capital, psycho-social aspects, each of which can impact on student experience and outcomes.

At the same time, there is a wide range of research that focuses on the HE experiences and outcomes of the different student cohorts constituting the split metric groups; students with disabilities (e.g. Griful-Freixenet, Struyven, Verstichele, & Andries, 2017; Hong, 2015), mature students (e.g. Bolam & Dodgson, 2003; Howard & Davies, 2013; Reay, 2002), BAME students (e.g. Caplan & Ford, 2014; Clegg, Parr, & Wan, 2003; Clegg & Stevenson, 2010; Cousin & Cureton, 2012; Dhanda, 2010; Mountford Zimdars et al. 2015; Stevenson, 2012).

From this varied literature emerges a complex system of contextual factors that impact in a variety of ways on the academic experiences and outcomes of different student groups. Taken as a whole, this body of work reveals the extent to which HE pedagogy is systemically heterogenic; student experience and outcomes vary according to differences between institutions or institution type; variations in the pedagogic or epistemic underpinnings of individual disciplines; the pedagogic approach of individual teaching staff; and the needs and learning approaches of different student cohorts. As Carnell and Fung (2017) observe, there are

> ...*huge numbers of variables at play [...] for example, in student demographics; in student prior learning experiences; in disciplinary and departmental contexts and cultures; in the communication styles and assumptions of those who are teaching or facilitating learning.*

> *(p. 3)*

Similarly, in her review of attempts to measure HE learning gain, Camille Kandiko Howson (2018) argues that 'learning is a complex phenomenon, and the multiple aspects of learning which students, institutions and other stakeholders are interested in means that there will be no "silver bullet" or single measure of learning gain' (p. 11). Even more damningly in the context of the TEF's approach to inclusion and equality issues via metrics, Greatbatch and Holland (2016) point out that

> *…there is no evidence on how teaching quality metrics can be broken down to different groups of learners, particularly groups differentiated by learner characteristics rather than subject / programme studied.*

> *(p. 70)*

And this is before the impact of intersectional factors are considered (Burke et al., 2013; Cotton, Joyner, George, & Cotton, 2016; Hockings, 2010; NUS 2011; Yosso, 2005). Under these conditions, it becomes clear just how complex and wide-ranging the issues feeding into and reflected in the individual TEF metrics are.

TEF AS A POLICY LEVER

Moreover, and in addition to the opacity of its assessment methodology and the complex construction of its various metrics, the leverage of TEF as a policy lever to drive institutional behaviour has other significant additional weaknesses built into its design:

- The causal relationships between the metrics and the desired outcomes (excellent teaching) are weak, with the guidance itself making an explicit acknowledgement that they are, at best, proxies for teaching quality (DBIS, 2016, p. 46).

- The relationship between the split metrics and the component metrics is complex. By effectively splitting core metrics several times, the impact of split metric performance on the overall core metric outcome is difficult to unpack.

- Prior to the roll-out of subject level TEF, assessment takes place at an aggregate level for the whole institution, meaning that high or low outlying results from a small number of departments could skew the overall results.

This complexity at the level of both structure and individual metrics exposes fundamental ambiguity about the role and function of TEF in contemporary HE policy. On (White) paper, the TEF is explicitly positioned as a mechanism to incentivise HE providers to deliver excellence in teaching to their students, and to do so inclusively (DBIS, 2016, p. 43). The use of incentives are components in a wide-ranging policy toolkit available to decision-makers (e.g. Linder & Peters, 1989; Vedung, 1998). Vedung (1998) boiled down a wide range of options to a tripartite model of incentives (carrots), regulation (sticks) and sermons (information). In these terms, the HE White Paper explicitly offers TEF as a carrot to HE providers. In its initial formulation, the TEF dangled the prospects of both a direct financial incentive (the ability to raise tuition fees in line with inflation) and an implied (albeit deferred) financial benefit, via reputational gains, which, translated into improved recruitment, would generate an increased volume of fees. As Vedung (1998) goes on to suggest, such incentivising policy instruments 'make it cheaper or more expensive in terms of money, time, effort, and other valuables to pursue certain actions' (p. 32). The recent decision to delink TEF outcomes with tuition fee inflation (Havergal, 2017), however, weakens its power as a financial incentive.

Crucially, policy incentives can be effective only when the outcomes they are designed to deliver are achievable and the delivery mechanisms required to achieve them are clear. Given its inherent complexity and the multiple points of indeterminacy/assessor judgement within the assessment framework and the individual metrics themselves, unpacking the opaque causal relationship between provider activities and assessment outcome/TEF ranking is likely to be challenging for most institutions, and particularly those with a mixed metric profile. Not for nothing did WonkHE, an online policy resource, refer to the TEF as an 'incredible machine' (WonkHE, 2018). Lacking a clear model for how they can affect their individual metrics, HE providers can have little or no practical leverage over their eventual TEF ranking (Baker, 2018; Barkas et al. 2019) and TEF's purpose as a mechanism to drive institutional behaviour in a particular direction is therefore deeply flawed.

COMPLEXITY AND 'WICKIDITY' AT THE LEVEL OF INDIVIDUAL METRICS

Moreover, the kinds of teaching quality and inclusive teaching issues for which the core and split TEF metrics (student satisfaction metrics, continuation rates, employability outcomes) are proxy measures, represent wicked problems for HE providers (Barkas et al. 2019; Zepke, 2018). In their paper on problem definition, Bore and Wright (2009) define a wicked problem as an issue that is 'not easily defined, has many causal levels and cannot be solved by generic principles or linear heuristics' (p. 242). They go on to suggest that problem design in public policy hinges on a distinction between

> *...on the one hand what is needed by government, i.e.*
> *electability, and on the other what can be done at the*
> *lowest level of policy implementation, what we have*
> *termed the micro level, by the social actors on the*
> *shop floor, the professionals and those for, and with,*
> *whom they work.*

(p. 244)

As I have discussed above, this problematises any attempt to position the TEF as a demonstration of genuine policy concern with social mobility, largely because of a lack of clarity about how policy implementation is to be enacted. Moreover, policymakers, as Bore and Wright (2009) suggest, often over-assume homogeneity and inflexibility in the populations they frame policy for. They conclude, therefore, that

> *...an absence of the recognition of key elements of*
> *social complexity can lead the policy developer and*
> *the professional practitioner into misunderstanding*
> *both the problem they wish to address and the*
> *possible 'solutions' they might apply.*

(p. 244)

This intrinsic complexity has clear issues for a policy lever intended simply to drive inclusive learning and teaching and 'excellence in teaching'.

STRATEGIC AMBIGUITY

Effective and clear solutions to the complex issues of inclusive learning and teaching are the deferred absences around which the TEF is framed. As such, the framework and its policy function rest on a strategic ambiguity, a common rhetorical technique. The reasons for deploying such ambiguity in policy discourses can be benign or manipulative.

At the benign end of the scale, Trowler (2003), for example, suggests that such uncertainty could result from 'the difficulty of making policies that will work; understanding causes and effects in the social world is extremely complex and "solutions" are not easy to find' (p. 112). Other commentators note that strategic ambiguity can serve to gloss over a range of stakeholder differences in approach or policy orientation and/or encourage creative collaboration (Davenport & Leitch, 2005) even in the face of conflicting goals or multiple perspectives (Abdallah & Langley, 2014; Leitch & Davenport, 2007). For Vedung (1997) obscure policy formation can conceal discord amongst policymakers, or conversely to conceal accord or even 'inopportune motivations' (p. 223).

A more cynical reading of strategic ambiguity suggests that it could be used to smooth over or conceal areas where no clear outcomes are possible (Jarzabkowski, Sillince, & Shaw, 2015). Indeed, Vedung (1997) suggests that policy obscurity can result from a policy framer's 'lack of time and knowledge' to engage with the complexities of the problem (p. 223). But as he goes on to observe, the result is often that 'policy indeterminateness shifts the responsibility for issuing specific rules from formal decision-makers to formal implementers and affected interest organizations' (p. 224). As such, strategic ambiguity enables policymakers to frame policy in ways that support politically expedient claims, such as to be addressing social inequality, whilst simultaneously sidestepping the need to address wicked implementation issues. In such cases, policy formation becomes a performative act designed to conceal the lack of easy solutions, as in, for example, the 'constructive ambiguity' deployed in the midst of the tortuously ambiguous Brexit negotiations between the UK government and EU representatives (Usherwood, 2017).

In this reading, it is the policymakers who, rather than wishing to make it so, are more concerned to be observed doing the wishing. Millward (2005), for example, notes that some policy announcements, when considered as speech acts, serve to obscure the gap between saying and doing. She highlights, as an example, verbs which 'sound performative but may not have much illocutionary effect', for example, 'we are tackling problems' or 'we are addressing the issue'. She notes that this is 'language which sounds as if it has illocutionary force – or as if something is being done' but without actually making it so (p. 602). This is the case, I suggest, with the statement from the White Paper, with which this chapter opened; 'we will enhance teaching in our universities by implementing the Teaching Excellence Framework' (DBIS, 2016, p. 19). This double practice, the gap between the saying and the doing, illuminates the distance between the performance of a policy concern and the actual realisation of its aims. Thus, the architects of the White Paper and TEF guidance tack backwards and forwards between their implicitly desired outcomes, the imposition of market logic and competition on the HE sector and a simultaneous need to play to expectations about social mobility and ethics, by making them explicit. From this perspective, wishing, as a speech act or performance, *is* the making it so, and as such the end in itself.

This is not, however, to suggest that such policy mobilisations do not have positive outcomes. Stephen Ball's (1993; 2015) work on policy 'ad hockery', suggests that there may be a space in which performative policy agendas can be subverted and used to advance a more progressive agenda. Ball's (2015) analysis of the way that school teachers resisted unwelcome policy impositions, helps unpick how this might work in practice by focusing on the 'mundane and quotidian *practices* of *policy translation* and *enactment* as these occur in the everyday life of schools' (p. 308). As Ball suggests 'the idea of resistance or perhaps more appropriately refusal, becomes a central aspect in the analysis of power relations and the struggle to produce identity and meaning within the structural and discursive limitations of everyday practice' (p. 310). In the same way, writing about the imposition of performativity in the learning and skills sector, Steer et al (2007) observe that practitioners might respond to policy levers by 'strategically' and even 'ingeniously' complying with 'the demands of external policy levers, whilst acting in accord with their own professional values and judgement' (p. 187).

From this perspective, the very unrealisability of the TEF, the blank space where solutions should be, provides an opportunity for learning and teaching practitioners inter-ested in developing more inclusive institutional approaches. The imposition of pressure on HE providers to respond to the challenges presented by the TEF metrics could force open fractures in organizational logics, in which opportunities for more inclusive learning and teaching practice could take root. The complex and context-dependent nature of the issues articulated in the TEF framework, and for which the metrics operate as poor proxies, mean that few institutions grappling with the implications of the TEF, will have ready solutions to hand. As such, the need to respond to the TEF forces HE providers to confront the highly localized contexts of individual practice, disciplinary differences and the diversity of students. This creates spaces and opportunities for individual practitioners to step in and offer their capacity for providing the localized and context-calibrated expertise required. In this way, progressive learning and teaching practitioners can co-opt and redirect the pressure exerted by the TEF, and by making a case for solutions rooted in their own practices in teaching excellence, take the opportunity to define how, in what contexts, and for whom it can be delivered.

REFERENCES

Abdallah, C., & Langley, A. (2014). The double edge of ambiguity in strategic planning. *Journal of Management Studies*, *51*(2), 235–264.

Baker, S. (2018). TEF results 2018: Performance on the metrics. Times Higher Education, June 6. Retrieved from https://www.timeshighereducation.com/blog/tef-results-2018-performance-metrics. Accessed on May 13, 2018.

Ball, S. (1993). What is policy? Texts, trajectories and toolboxes. *Discourse: Studies in the Cultural Politics of Education*, *13*(2), 10–17.

Ball, S. (2012). Performativity, commodification and commitment: An I-spy guide to the neoliberal university. *British Journal of Educational Studies*, *60*(1), 17–28.

Ball, S. (2015). What is policy? 21 years later: Reflections on the possibilities of policy research. *Discourse: Studies in the Cultural Politics of Education*, *36*(3), 306–313.

Ball, S. (2016). Neoliberal education? Confronting the slouching beast. *Policy Futures in Education*, *14*(8), 1046–1059.

Ball, S., Maguire, M., Braun, A., Perryman, J., & Hoskins, K. (2012). Assessment technologies in schools: 'deliverology' and the 'play of dominations'. *Research Papers in Education*, *27*(5), 513–533.

Barber, M. (2011). *Deliverology 101: A field guide for educational leaders*. London: SAGE Publications.

Barkas, L., Scott, J., Poppitt, N., & Smith, P. (2019). Tinker, tailor, policy-maker: Can the UK government's teaching excellence framework deliver its objectives? *Journal of Further and Higher Education*, *43*(6), 801–813.

Bell, A., & Brooks, C. (2018). What makes students satisfied? A discussion and analysis of the UK's national student survey. *Journal of Further and Higher Education*, *42*(8), 1118–1142.

Bennett, R., & Kane, S. (2014). Students' interpretations of the meanings of questionnaire items in the National Student Survey. *Quality in Higher Education*, *20*(2), 129–164.

Bessant, S., Robinson, Z., & Ormerod, M. (2015). Neoliberalism, new public management and the sustainable development agenda of higher, education: History, contradictions and synergies. *Environmental Education Research*, *21*(3), 417–432.

Blackmore, J. (2009). Academic pedagogies, quality logics and performative universities: Evaluating teaching and what students want. *Studies in Higher Education*, *34*(8), 857–872.

Bolam, H., & Dodgson, R. (2003). Retaining and supporting mature students in higher education. *Journal of Adult and Continuing Education*, *8*(2), 179–194.

Bore, A., & Wright, N. (2009). The wicked and complex in education: Developing a transdisciplinary perspective for policy formulation, implementation and professional practice. *Journal of Education for Teaching*, *35*(3), 241–256.

Bovill, C., Cook-Sather, A., Felton, P., Millard, L., & Moore-Cherry, N. (2016). Addressing potential challenges in co-creating learning and teaching: Overcoming resistance, navigating institutional norms and ensuring inclusivity in student–staff partnerships. *Higher Education*, *71*, 195–208.

Bowl, M. (2019). Diversity and differentiation, equity and equality in a marketised higher education system. In M. Bowl, C. McCaig, & J. Hughes (Eds.), *Equality and differentiation in marketised higher education* (pp. 1–19). London: Palgrave Macmillan.

Burke, P., Crozier, G., Read, B., Hall, J., Peat, J., & Francis, B. (2013). *Formations of gender and higher education pedagogies (GaP)* (pp. 1–61), York: Higher Education Academy.

Canning, J. (2019). The UK Teaching Excellence Framework (TEF) as an illustration of Baudrillard's hyperreality. *Discourse: Studies in the Cultural Politics of Education*, *40*(3), 319–330.

Caplan, P., & Ford, J. (2014). Voices of diversity: What students of diverse races/ethnicities and both sexes tell us about their perceptions about their institutions progress towards diversity. *Aporia*, *6*(3), 30–69.

Carnell, B., & Fung, D. (2017). Editors Introduction. In B. Carnell & D. Fung (Eds.), *Developing the higher education curriculum: Research-based education in practice* (pp. 1–13). London: UCL Press.

Clegg, S., Parr, S., & Wan, S. (2003). Racialising discourses in higher education. *Teaching in Higher Education*, *8*(2), 155–168.

Clegg, S., & Stevenson, J. (2010). *An exploration of the link between 'possible selves' and the attainment of BME students on social science courses*. Leeds: Leeds Metropolitan University.

Cocksedge, S., & Taylor, D. (2013). The national student survey: Is it just a bad DREEM? *Medical Teacher, 35*(12), 1638–1643.

Cotton, D., Joyner, M., George, R., & Cotton, P. (2016). Understanding the gender and ethnicity attainment gap in UK higher education. *Innovations in Education & Teaching International, 53*(5), 475–486.

Cousin, G., & Cureton, D. (2012). *Disparities in student attainment*. York: Higher Education Academy and Equalities Challenge Unit.

Davenport, S., & Leitch, S. (2005). Circuits of power in practice: Strategic ambiguity as delegation of authority. *Organization Studies, 26*(11), 1603–1623.

Department of Business, Innovation and Skills (DBIS). (2016). *Success as a knowledge economy: Teaching excellence, social mobility and student choice*. London: DBIS.

Department for Education (DfE). (2017). *Teaching excellence and student outcomes framework specification*. London: DfE.

Dhanda, M. (2010). Understanding disparities in student attainment: Black and minority ethnic students' experience. University of Wolverhampton. Retrieved from http://www2.wlv.ac.uk/equalopps/mdsummary.pdf. Accessed on May 1, 2019.

Forstenzer, J. (2016). The teaching excellence framework: What's the purpose? Report. The Crick Centre for Engaged Philosophy and the University of Sheffield.

Frankham, J. (2017). Employability and higher education: The follies of the 'productivity challenge' in the teaching excellence framework. *Journal of Education Policy*, *32*(5), 628–641.

Gillard, J. (2018). An initial analysis and reflection of the metrics used in the Teaching Excellence Framework in the UK. Perspectives: Policy and Practice in Higher Education, *22*(2), 49–57.

Giroux, H. (2014). *Neoliberalism's war on higher education*. Chicago, IL: Haymarket Books.

Greatbatch, D., & Holland, J. (2016). *Teaching quality in higher education: Literature review and qualitative research*. London: DBIS.

Green, F., & Kynaston, D. (2019). Britain's private school problem: it's time to talk. *The Observer*, January 13. Retrieved from https://www.theguardian.com/education/2019/jan/13/public-schools-david-kynaston-francis-green-engines-of-privilege. Accessed on May 1, 2019.

Griful-Freixenet, J., Struyven, K., Verstichele, M., & Andries, C. (2017). Higher education students with disabilities speaking out: Perceived barriers and opportunities of the Universal Design for Learning framework. *Disability & Society*, *32*(10), 1627–1649.

Gunn, A. (2018). Metrics and methodologies for measuring teaching quality in higher education: Developing the teaching excellence framework (TEF). *Educational Review*, *70*(2), 129–148.

Gunn, V., & Fisk, A. (2013). *Considering teaching excellence in higher education: 2007–2013: A literature review since the CHERI report 2007*, York: Higher Education

Academy. Retrieved from http://eprints.gla.ac.uk/87987/1/87987.pdf. Accessed on May 10, 2018.

Hall, W. (2013). Consumerism and consumer complexity: Implications for university teaching and teaching evaluation. *Nurse Education Today*, *33*(7), 720–723.

Harvey, D. (2007). *A brief history of neoliberalism*. Oxford: Oxford University Press.

Havergal, C. (2017). House of lords rejects plans to link TEF results to tuition fees. *High*, March 6. Retrieved from https://www.timeshighereducation.com/news/house-lords-rejects-plans-link-tef-results-tuition-fees. Accessed on May 1, 2019.

Hockings, C. (2010). *Inclusive learning and teaching in higher education: A synthesis of research*. York: Higher Education Academy.

Holloway, J., & Brass, J. (2018). Making accountable teachers: The terrors and pleasures of performativity. *Journal of Education Policy*, *33*(3), 361–382.

Hong, B. (2015). Qualitative analysis of the barriers college students with disabilities experience in higher education. *Journal of College Student Development*, *56*(3), 209–226.

Hood, C. (1995). The 'new public management' in the 1980s: Variations on a theme. *accounting, Organizations and Society*, *20*(2/3), 93–109.

Howard, C., & Davies, P. (2013). Attracting mature students into higher education: The impact of approaches to learning and social identity. *Journal of Further and Higher Education*, *37*(6), 769–785.

Howson, C. (2018). *Evaluation of HEFCE's learning gain pilot projects year* (Vol. 2). Bristol: HEFCE.

Ingleby, E. (2015). The house that Jack built: Neoliberalism, teaching in higher education and the moral objections. *Teaching in Higher Education, 20*(5), 518–529.

Jarzabkowski, P., Sillince, J. A., & Shaw, D. (2015). Strategic ambiguity as a rhetorical resource for enabling multiple interests. *Human Relations, 63*(2), 219–248.

Johnsen, A. (2005). What does 25 years of experience tell us about the state of performance measurement in public policy and management? *Public Money & Management, 25*(1), 9–17.

Jones, G. (2013). Afterword: Rates of exchange: Neoliberalism and the value of higher education. *International Studies in Sociology of Education, 23*(3), 273–280.

Leitch, S., & Davenport, S. (2007). Strategic ambiguity as a discourse practice: The role of keywords in the discourse on "sustainable" biotechnology. *Discourse Studies, 9*(1), 43–61.

Linder, S., & Peters, B. (1989). Instruments of government: Perceptions and contexts. *Journal of Public Policy, 9*(1), 35–58.

Mahony, P., & Weiner, G. (2019). Neo-liberalism and the state of higher education in the UK. *Journal of Further and Higher Education, 43*(4), 560–572.

Marginson, S. (2006). Dynamics of national and global competition in higher education. *Higher Education, 52*, 1–39.

Marginson, S. (2011). Higher education and public good. *Higher Education Quarterly, 65*(4), 53–69.

Marginson, S. (2013). The impossibility of capitalist markets in higher education. *Journal of Education Policy, 28*(3), 353–370.

McCaig, C. (2016). The retreat from widening participation? The national scholarship programme and new access agreements in English higher education. *Studies in Higher Education*, *41*(2), 215–230.

McCaig, C. (2019). English higher education: Widening participation and the historical context for system differentiation. In M, Bowl, C. McCaig, & J. Hughes (Eds.), *Equality and differentiation in marketised higher education* (pp. 50–72). London: Palgrave Macmillan.

Millward, L. (2005). "We are announcing your target": Reflections on performative language in the making of English housing policy. *Local Government Studies*, *31*(5), 597–614.

Moore, J., Higham, L., & Sanders, J. (2018). *Evidencing teaching excellence: Analysis of the teaching excellence framework (TEF2) provider submissions*. York: Higher Education Academy.

Morrison, A., Cannella, G., & Koro-Ljungberg, M. (2017). The responsibilized consumer: Neoliberalism and English higher education policy. *Cultural Studies – Critical Methodologies*, *17*(3), 197–204.

Mount-Zimdars, A., Sabri, D., Moore, J., Sanders, J., Jones, S., & Higham, L. (2015). *Causes of differences in student outcomes*, London: HEFCE, pp. 1–132.

National Union of Students (NUS). (2011). *Race for equality: A report on the experiences of black students in further and higher education*. London: NUS. Retrieved from https://www.nus.org.uk/PageFiles/12238/NUS_Race_for_Equality_web.pdf. Accessed on May 10, 2019.

Nixon, E., Scullion, R., & Hearn, R. (2018). Her majesty the student: Marketised higher education and the narcissistic (dis)satisfactions of the student-consumer. *Studies in Higher Education*, *43*(6), 927–943.

Nordstrum, L., LeMahieu, P, & Dodd, K. (2017). Deliverology. *Quality Assurance in Education*, *25*(1), 43–57.

Olssen, M., & Peters, M. (2005). Neoliberalism, higher education and the knowledge economy: From the free market to knowledge capitalism. *Journal of Education Policy*, *20*(3), 313–345.

Parker, C., & Mathews, B. (2001). Customer satisfaction: Contrasting academic and consumers' interpretations. *Marketing Intelligence & Planning*, *19*(1), 38–44.

Polkinghorne, M., Roushan, G., & Taylor, J. (2017). Considering the marketing of higher education: The role of student learning gain as a potential indicator of teaching quality. *Journal of Marketing for Higher Education*, *27*(2), 213–232.

Pusser, B., & Marginson, S. (2013). University rankings in critical perspective. *Journal of Higher Education*, *84*(4), 544–568.

Rand, A. (1989). *The voice of reason: Essays in objectivist thought*. Peikoff, L. (Ed.), New York, NY: Penguin.

Reay, D. (2002). Class, authenticity and the transition to higher education for mature students. *The Sociological Review*, *50*(3), 398–418.

Riddell, R. (2013). Changing policy levers under the neoliberal state: Realising coalition policy on education and social mobility. *Journal of Education Policy*, *28*(6), 847–863.

Sabri, D. (2011). What's wrong with 'the student experience'? *Discourse: Studies in the Cultural Politics of Education*, *32*(5), 657–667.

Sabri, D. (2013). Student Evaluations of Teaching as 'Fact-Totems': The Case of the UK National Student Survey. *Sociological Research Online*, *18*(4), 1–15.

Sarrico, C., Rosa, M., Teixeira, P., & Cardoso, M. (2010). Assessing quality and evaluating performance in higher education: Worlds apart or complementary views? *Minerva Special Issue: Universities in the new knowledge landscape*, *48*(1), 35–54.

Savigny, H. (2013). The (political) idea of a university: Political science and neoliberalism in English higher education. *European Political Science*, *12*, 432–439.

Steer, R., Spours, K., Hodgson, A., Finlay, I., Coffield, F., Edward, S., & Gregson, M. (2007). 'Modernisation' and the role of policy levers in the learning and skills sector. *Journal of Vocational Education and Training*, *59*(2), 175–192.

Stevenson, J. (2012). *Black and minority ethnic student degree retention and attainment*. York: Higher Education Academy.

The Student Survey.com. (2018). National student survey 2017 – core questionnaire. Retrieved from https://www.thestudent survey.com/content/NSS2017_Core_Questionnaire.pdf. Accessed on May 13, 2018.

Tomlinson, M., Enders, J., & Naidoo, R. (2018). The teaching excellence framework: Symbolic violence and the measured market in higher education. *Critical Studies in Education*, 1–16.

Trow, M. (1973). *Problems in the transition from elite to mass higher education*. Berkeley, CA: Carnegie Commission on Higher Education.

Trowler, P. (2003). *Education policy: A policy sociology approach* (2nd ed.). London: Routledge.

Usherwood, S. (2017, December 5). Regulatory alignment, constructive ambiguity and Brexit. Political Studies Association. Retrieved from https://www.psa.ac.uk/psa/news/regulatory-alignment-constructive-ambiguity-and-brexit. Accessed on May 1, 2019.

Vedung, E. (1997). *Public policy and programme evaluation.* London: Transaction Publishers.

Vedung, E. (1998). Policy instruments: Typologies and theories. In L. Bemelmans-Videc, R. Rist, & E. Vedung (Eds.), *Carrots, Sticks and sermons: Policy instruments and their evaluation* (pp. 21–58). London: Transaction Publishers.

WonkHE, (2018). TEF: The incredible Machine remixed. Retrieved from https://wonkhe.com/blogs/the-incredible-machine-remixed/. Accessed on May 13, 2018.

Woodall, T., Hiller, A., & Resnick, S. (2014). Making sense of higher education: Students as consumers and the value of the university experience. *Studies in Higher Education, 39*(1), 48–67.

Yorke, M. (2009). 'Student experience' surveys: Some methodological considerations and an empirical investigation. *Assessment & Evaluation in Higher Education, 34*(6), 721–739.

Yosso, T. (2005). Whose culture has capital? A critical race theory discussion of community cultural wealth. *Race, Ethnicity and Education, 8*(1), 69–91.

Zepke, N. (2018). Student engagement in neo-liberal times: What is missing? *Higher Education Research and Development, 37*(2), 433–446.

4

RAPPORT AND RELATIONSHIPS: THE STUDENT PERSPECTIVE ON TEACHING EXCELLENCE

Jenny Lawrence, Hollie Shaw, Leanne Hunt, and Donovan Synmoie

ABSTRACT

This chapter attempts to capture what teaching excellence looks and feels like for students. Our research reports on research conducted by two student authors at separate institutions. It suggests that the most crucial aspect of the student experience of 'teaching excellence' is a teacher's ability to build rapport and create meaningful interpersonal relationships with their students. Leanne Hunt's research was conducted with her fellow students at the University of Bradford. She outlines how, for her participants, the student–teacher rapport informed a positive learning experience which translated into a mutual understanding of excellent teaching. Widening participation, college-based HE student Hollie Shaw, now at Sheffield Hallam University, defines teaching excellence as flexible enough to respond to student learning needs, but strong enough to inspire interest in the discipline. In this

*chapter, we consider their separate testimonies carefully:
we argue that exploring unconscious bias furthers
understanding of how differences between student and
teacher may compromise interpersonal relations and so
student recognition of a tutor's positive and crucial role in
the student experience and the implications of how one
might measure this given the emphasis on proxies for
teaching excellence in the TEF. We suggest breaking
down unconscious bias calls for embracing differences,
reflection and recognising the complexities of contemporary staff and student university lives. This chapter's
exploration of staff–student partnership opens up potential for the creation of more equitable and honest learning
dynamics in higher education – where a nuanced understanding of 'teaching excellence' can be defined, understood and evidenced within a HEI, with external bodies
such as the Office for Students, and included in the
Teaching Excellence Framework.*

Keywords: Student perspectives; unconscious bias;
evaluation; rapport; learning relationships; teaching
enhancement framework

INTRODUCTION

Student–authors here suggest that a teacher's ability to create
a meaningful interpersonal relationship with them is crucial
to experiencing 'teaching excellence', and, taking this on
board, consider more meaningful ways of understanding and
capturing what teaching excellence looks and feels like.

The authors met at the 2017 Staff and Educational Developers Association annual conference. Hollie and Leanne were
giving inaugural student keynotes and Jenny, an academic
developer, sponsored Hollie's paper. Donovan Synmoie, an

academic developer, was a delegate. This coauthored chapter is based on Hollie and Leanne's separate presentations and our subsequent conversations about rapport and the relationships between students and their teachers and what teaching excellence means to students. Leanne's research, conducted with students at the University of Bradford, explores how mutual teacher–student rapport informs a positive learning experience (Hunt, 2017). Widening participation student Hollie reflects on her experience as a student at University Centre, North Lindsey College, and defines teaching excellence as flexible and inspiring (Shaw, 2017). Donovan and Jenny consider the implications for staff of these student testimonies. Finally, Jenny charts the evolution of our thinking about teaching excellence. Where authors speak directly to the reader their words are in italics.

This chapter outlines the ways in which implications for teachers from groups underrepresented in HE such as working class, LGBQT and black, Asian and minority ethnic HE teachers, may experience barriers to creating meaningful interpersonal relationships with students because of student unconscious bias, which, we argue, along with other contributors to the collection, may translate into compromised student evaluation and the metrics that inform TEF. This chapter concludes with a hopeful consideration of how the issue of diversity, difference and unconscious bias identified may be mitigated through a united will to learn and the creation of 'rapport' that in turn foster positive teaching and learning experiences which could be used to more meaningfully evaluate notions of teaching excellence.

The terms 'teacher' and 'staff' are used throughout this chapter to mean lecturers, tutors, supervisors and professional/support service staff involved in facilitating student learning (staff often excluded from discussions about teaching – yet play a crucial role in student learning experiences).

We draw on a view expressed by the NUS in their open letter in response to TEF, where they suggest they would 'rather help develop an approach that is based on partnership between students and staff; using better means of measuring and tracking quality enhancement' than the given 'question-able metrics' (NUS, 2016). The NUS Partnership Manifesto (2015) has at its heart unity and equality between staff and students. The Manifesto argues against measuring student satisfaction based only on feedback from individual students, recognising this 'sits neatly in a consumer model' (NUS, 2015, p. 8) which merely 'offers a false and inflated perception of their own power' (NUS, 2015, p. 5). Rather, they advocate a self-conscious effort to create equitable relationships between students and teachers and 'break down the barriers' (NUS, 2015, p. 14) to partnership working. We explore the impor-tance of learning relationships and how barriers to rapport between students and their tutors can be navigated.

INTERPERSONAL RELATIONSHIPS

As discussed elsewhere in this collection, a lack of consensus of what 'teaching excellence' means makes it hard to define (Gunn & Fisk, 2013) and measure (Blackmore, Blackwell, & Edmondson, 2016; French & O'Leary, 2017). However, the importance of a teacher's personal attributes as integral to teaching excellence is widely recognised: 'Excellent teachers bring their own experiences and identity into teaching and are emotionally invested in their students' outcomes' (Rigby, 2017). This chapter, based on qualitative, focus group research with fellow students exploring the value of staff–student rapport at Bradford Leanne (Hunt, 2017), echoes this sentiment. Her findings suggest an educator's social interactions with students, or rapport, is crucial to students' perception of teaching excellence. Leanne concludes from her research that HE teachers and students should be helped to respect and recognise the social, cultural and professional context they both inhabit in order to build a meaningful interpersonal relationship and so acknowledge what is valuable in teaching and learning. This, we argue in this chapter, is crucial to academic success (Hunt, 2017, p. 2), and should lead to a more nuanced understanding and experience of excellent teaching.

Student–teacher rapport/relationships are central to effective learning (hooks, 2010; Hunt, 2017; Shaw, 2017).[1] Interpersonal relations within a learning community (student-to-student, student-to-teacher, teacher-to-teacher) create an inclusive, productive learning environment and foster for students a sense of belonging understood to affect retention, success and wellbeing (Haughton & Anderson, 2017; Thomas, 2012). This is particularly important for widening participation students who often experience alienation (Thomas, 2012) and black, Asian and ethnic minority students who may feel 'out of place' (Bhopal, 2018, p. 92).

Student Perspectives on Teaching Excellence: Rapport

The research that informs this paper tells us student–teacher rapport can significantly influence a student's learning experience and outcomes (Wilson, Ryan, & Pugh, 2010). A recent study of student perception of teaching excellence found students place the relationship with their teacher over academic content (Lammers, Gillaspy, & Hancock, 2017). Rapport, in this sense, has been defined as 'interaction with components of friendliness and care (Altman, 1990)' (Hunt, 2017, p. 2), and is central to the initial development of any relationship

---

1 bell hooks does not use capitals in her name.

(Smith, 2015). Vygotsky claimed that learning is enhanced by student–teacher connection, where deep learning is experienced as a collaborative journey (Clapper, 2015). However, teaching excellence as it is measured in the metrics that inform TEF does not capture the importance of the learning relationships understood as central to a positive learning experience (Wood & O'Leary, 2019).

Leanne Hunt: Rapport and Relationships at the University of Bradford

The University of Bradford has approximately 10,000 students. To explore how to improve engagement with our students' extra-curricular Peer Assisted Learning (PAL) scheme whilst a student I conducted a qualitative study, using focus groups, to explore student understanding of staff-student rapport. Although small scale, the depth and quality of data offered useful findings about the impact of rapport on a student's perspective of teaching excellence.

Participants were recruited via an email call to those involved with the PAL scheme. They were a mixed gender group from a variety of backgrounds, some were widening participation students, the first group were in their first- and second years of study, and second in their third. University ethical processes were followed and participants gave informed consent to use findings in academic outputs. Focus group data was interrogated using manual coded thematic analysis.

Participants, when asked what their PAL leaders did to build rapport, led the discussion to issues around rapport with course teachers. Participants defined rapport in teaching and learning context as small social graces that nurtured connection, such as knowing their name, which course of study they were on, and relating to them on professional and personal levels, for example asking how studies were going or the school run went.

This recognition of the students' particular context (a carer, a worker), and the demands on their energies outside the classroom was central to participants experience of rapport. Similarly, students appreciated insight into their teacher's life outside the classroom e.g. a teacher who explained they needed to leave a class promptly to attend a meeting.

Further, participants reported that teachers who created laughter in their classroom built the most meaningful relationships with their students.

Participants felt that when the rapport described was established, when they felt connected to their teacher they enjoyed: a richer learning experience, which led to higher marks; increased academic confidence; motivation to attend; confidence in both their teachers and the University; an overall increase in self-esteem.

Participants understood 'lack of rapport' as when a teacher "only stand there and teach", teachers who "don't relate to students" in a personal way and who only discussed the class subject-matter. One student explained "there's no trust built up they just come in stand in front of ya they deliver the lecture". When studying with teachers who did not build rapport, students reported they were less likely to attend and made clear "I engage more in the sessions that I've got rapport from the lecturer". Participants reported that lack of rapport felt like being an anonymous member of a group and led to lower assessment grades.

Hollie Shaw: Student-Centred Teaching and Interpersonal Relationships at the University Centre, North Lindsey College

Feng and Wood (2012) found three main factors influence student perception of teaching: subject knowledge; lessons delivered; and willingness to help students. This resonates for me as a widening participation student. In my SEDA conference paper I defined teaching excellence as teaching flexible enough to respond to student learning needs, but robust enough to inspire interest in the discipline (Shaw, 2017).

I enrolled at The University Centre, North Lindsey College in 2015 as a mature student. The University Centre delivers programmes validated by several University partners to approximately 1,500 widening participation undergraduates, all drawn from the local region, which has a Participation of local students (POLAR) rating of 1, the lowest quintile of the POLAR rating (Office for Students, 2019)- I was the first in my family to study in HE and had young children to care for. However, during my time at The University Centre, I was able to excel both academically and in extracurricular activities. This success can, I feel, be attributed to the University Centre's institutional and pedagogical flexibility (Barnet, 2014), which underpins their student-centred ethos.

The University Centre instituted various student-centred practices which I found helpful. I had academic support in regular, scheduled meetings with subject teachers to discuss my progress or through an open-door policy. This open-door policy means that teachers were available to me at a time that suited me and my family. Staff were committed to offering individualised support, working with me until I felt confident in my understanding of the subject, however long that may take. This is a significant investment of the teacher's time and energy, and facilitated meaningful and close interpersonal relationships between me and my tutors.

This pedagogical approach is student centred and flexible. Based on my and other student's feedback teachers adapted delivery to accommodate our preference, for example, introducing formative assessments on our request, so students and teachers can together identify areas on which to focus. Learning technologies facilitates flexible teaching and learning

(Gordon, 2014). The University Centre made sure all students could access learning technologies by providing us with iPads. Disciplinary teachers adapted course materials to suit our learning needs, and curated extensive, accessible disciplinary resources to ignite our imagination.

The iPad provided meant I could access learning materials, engage in discussion with the learning community and contact teachers at times that worked around my personal commitments. This flexibility, and response to my needs assured I was able to deeply engage with the course content which proved crucial to my success. The individualised support I received built my confidence. With my teachers' student-centred approach and their personal investment in my success I was motivated to study harder. I wanted to make them proud of me and my work, as much as to realise the academic ambition their knowledge and enthusiasm for the subject instilled in me. I found excellent teaching in strong, inspiring teachers, who showed me they were equally invested in my academic journey.

The student centred ethos is bearing results for the college: in 2017, The University Centre was awarded TEF: Silver. In the outcome report from the TEF panel, the engagement between student and staff was highlighted as an area of excellence. The 2018 NSS score for 'I am able to contact staff when I needed to' scored 82%; and 79% for 'I have received sufficient advice and guidance on my course'.

BARRIERS TO BUILDING INTERPERSONAL RELATIONSHIPS IN THE HE CLASSROOM

The student perspectives Leanne and Hollie present although from quite different institutions (university and college HE), and with different evidence bases (Qualitative research and reflection), place the teacher–student relationships and a sense of rapport central to their learning experience and understanding of how a teacher is enhancing and transforming the student learning experience, and are reflected in data that contribute to TEF – the NSS. However, the NSS does not fully reflect the importance of rapport to the student experience.

Hollie and Leanne's shared understanding of the import of interpersonal relationships in teaching and learning brings hooks' (2003, 2010) work to mind. Rapport offers a way of creating a meaningfully transformative, critical pedagogy, they, like hooks suggests, recognise the importance of learning communities founded on equal and personal relationships between student and teacher. This equality is bound up in recognising each other's situatedness, particularity and common goal – the academic endeavour. hooks also makes a case for the politically and emotionally engaged educator as a transformative agent in the student's journey to self-actualisation, suggesting that this breaking down of the public and private persona to create a more equitable student–staff relations realises the notion of the personal as political (hooks, 2003).

However, the notion and subjective evidencing of more equitable and emotionally connected student–teacher interpersonal relationships is troubled by contemporary stressors across Higher Education in general, and on academic staff in particular.

Structural Impediments, Personal Boundaries and Identity

There are structural impediments to teachers building the rapport described with students: contemporary HE teachers often have a teaching portfolio so vast engaging with every member of the learning community is impossible (Morrish, 2019; Universities and Colleges Union, 2016). They may be compromised in building student relationships by other institutional pressures or workload, where personal wellbeing is compromised meaningful connection with the students may be interrupted (Lawrence, 2017b; Lawrence & Herrick, 2019; Morrish, 2019). Further, what of the teacher who would prefer to leave their private life outside of the classroom?

Diversity and Difference

The globalised, diversified higher education sector presents to the student a vast array of difference: people, social practices, ways of being and academic perspectives. This variety is arguably one of HE's greatest strengths: it presents a cultural richness and breadth of experience integral to the higher learning experience. Although HEIs are obliged to attend to equality, diversity and inclusion through the Equality Act 2010, legally bound interventions (equality and diversity impact assessments of policy and process, mandatory training) and sophisticated information, advice and guidance (available from respected national bodies such as Advance HE and Universities UK), they have not resolved inequalities across the sector. There is still a white-male domination of senior positions and professorial roles in HE; women and minorities are behind men in pay scales and sector standing (Bhopal, 2018). The Equality Act 2010 has not wiped out exclusive practices in HE, or, important here, successfully addressed the deeply complex issue of unconscious bias.

Jenny Lawrence and Donovan Synmoie: Unconscious Bias in Teaching Evaluations

The Equality Challenge Unit defines unconscious bias as 'bias we are unaware of, and which happens outside of our control.

It is bias that happens automatically and is triggered by our
brain making quick judgements and assessments of people and
situations, influenced by our background, cultural environment and personal experiences' (Equality Challenge Unit,
2013).

Much of the work on equality and diversity in HE reads
bias as working within clearly defined and understood hier-
archies of power such as the relationship between the
employing institution to the employee, the teaching institution
and staff to the student, and student to student-from-under-
represented-group/s. However, there is growing interest in
how student bias may be at play in the evaluation of HE
teaching, as discussed in chapter 6.

We are concerned unconscious bias may compromise student experience and expectation of rapport with staff from
under-represented groups in the same way as latent prejudice
compromises teacher evaluations (Boring, Ottoboni, & Stark,
2016) and perceived race and gender shapes student expectations of a teacher's practice (Criado-Perez, 2019; Reid,
2010). For example, students are more critical of female
teachers if they do not receive pastoral support than male
counterparts (Mitchell & Martin, 2018). We must ask: are
expectations higher for female staff to exhibit 'friendliness and
care' than their male counterparts? And, as Leanne notes,
students associate lack of rapport with their own attainment.
We must ask how is this reflected in teaching evaluation?

The research and reflections from students presented in this
chapter and understanding of the current HE terrain highlight
the potentially inexhaustible list of factors that may affect
student-teacher interpersonal relations; not only compromises
the students' learning experiences, but also have serious
implications for student evaluation of the staff teaching them.

The notion that unconscious bias may interrupt staff-
student rapport has far reaching consequences for the

institution: student perception of a lack of interpersonal relations temper NSS responses, the NSS informs TEF, TEF informs the various university rankings, rankings impact subsequent enrolments. The issue of student-teacher rapport/ relations is critical to student and institutional success. In America student assessment of their HE teachers is closing down opportunity for teachers from protected groups (Mitchell & Martin, 2018) as universities favour staff with more 'acceptable' personal profiles – with a mind to gaming the evaluations. In the UK, where personal characteristics predict academic career trajectory (Bhopal, 2018), we are concerned opportunities will be similarly arrested for some staff.

We also ask how far are teachers identified as lacking, when on closer investigation, it is the institution because of unrealistic workloads (Ahmed, 2017; Morrish, 2019; University and College Union, 2016), and wider sector values that puts teaching behind research in prestige and resource (Blackmore, Blackwell & Edmondson, 2016). All of which culminates in a work environment that often neglects to provide a setting where staff are able to build rapport and create meaningful interpersonal relationships with their students.

Jenny Lawrence: Transcending Difference and Diversity in Pursuit of Teaching Excellence

If we cannot dismantle TEF what can we do?

Freire tells us we are 'conditioned beings but not determined beings' (Freire, 2007, p. 37), can we then recalibrate unconscious bias and open up the potential to build rapport across diverse learning communities? Freire's openness to change, to new ideas drives a belief in the transformative force of higher learning. Radical openness (hooks, 1994) to new ways of thinking can start to address unconscious bias. To break down bias we must embrace our differences, and reflect deep within ourselves to recognise, and fully own our prejudices (Freire, 2007; hooks, 1994; Equality Challenge Unit, 2013). Even the most 'fair-minded' will benefit from such an exercise (Equality Challenge Unit, 2013, p. 4). We must ask ourselves how this can be done effectively. The student testimonies presented here, which prioritise rapport, may offer a hopeful response to new ways of formulating and capturing teaching excellence.

A Partnership Approach

The issue of power is crucial. Deconstructing hierarchical student–teacher relations is underpinned by democratic principles (Freire, 2004; hooks, 2010) that current student–staff partnership models embrace, for example, the NUS Manifesto for Partnership (2015) and student–staff partnership in educational development (Akhtar, 2018; Mathias & Peters, 2018). The active recognition of the concept of rapport as a shared student–teacher endeavour could help contemporary HE to find different ways to conduct teaching evaluation and create an alternative conception of teaching excellence.

Some universities have attempted to address unconscious bias by raising the issue on evaluation forms (see, for example, Flaherty, 2019); however, we suggest HEIs take active responsibility to 'create an atmosphere of openness in discussing biases and best practice to minimise them' (Muneer, Cotton, & Winter 2015) as an integral part of conducting teaching evaluation and building rapport between staff and students. We believe we are morally obligated to have

difficult, consciousness-raising conversations and, importantly, create more critically reflective and inclusive spaces for
dialogue about what forms the teacher–student relationship
could/should take; a dialogue where we can better understand
staff and student working contexts in order to facilitate
rapport.

Leanne Hunt: Students and Teachers Building Rapport

I graduated and am now working in professional services at
the University of Bradford, coordinating the PAL Scheme.
Inspired by Smith (2015) and Starcher (2011) I make a
conscious effort to build interpersonal learning relationships
with my students. To establish rapport I deploy the 'small
social graces' discussed above that students' value and reveal
to students aspects of my personal and professional self: I
explain I graduated only recently so can relate to the challenges they face; try to create a less formal dynamic; share
select details about my personal life; and say a casual hello
when I see my students outside the classroom. Students
reciprocate in kind - creating rapport.

This mutual relationship brings reward: student feedback is
positive; commitment to the voluntary PAL scheme stable;
students report they enjoy my sessions and consider me supportive; I enjoy my work. I am building a collegiate culture:
students are taking care to build rapport with their peers.
Students comment, in NSS free text responses, how participating in PAL has been central to their success. The University
of Bradford's TEF submission cited PAL as good practice:
Bradford won a Silver TEF award in 2017.

Becoming a member of staff has made me aware of the
difficulties faced in delivering teaching excellence, working
with ever increasing workloads and lack of resources is hard.
However, my being so close to the students [as a recent

graduate] does help me understand their needs, and helps me in my role - students feedback on my practice makes clear I have a positive impact on their learning.

Hollie Shaw: Students and Teachers Understanding Each Other's Working Context

I am now at Sheffield Hallam University, I have completed an integrated masters programme and am about to start a PhD This informs my new perspective and insight to the pressures teachers face in creating rapport. I recognised there may be structural barriers that interrupt the provision of individualised learning support and the building of interpersonal relationships. When first arriving at the university I was often one of 90 students in a lecture, which is quite different from my college HE experiences. Now in my second year at University, I have built better interpersonal relationships with many of my teachers, in part because I am considered a member of a research team. I have seen first-hand the volume and pace of teachers' work - in and outside the classroom, and the detrimental effect this has on their wellbeing, which inevitably affects teaching practice (Lawrence, 2017b; Lawrence & Herrick, 2019). I now recognise that my previous relationships with teachers were not equal - my tutors acknowledged the context in which I worked, but I did not recognise, or know anything about, theirs.

Jenny Lawrence, Hollie Shaw and Leanne Hunt: Students and Teachers United in the Will to Evidence Excellent Teaching

The brute metrics that inform TEF cannot in their current form capture the elements of teaching excellence students find meaningful - such as rapport (Wood and O'Leary, 2019). Furthermore those metrics work against staff from protected groups, or practicing in compromised circumstances.

We suggest teacher-student co-authoring of TEF institutional narratives offers opportunity to create a more nuanced approach to evidencing, rather than measuring, teaching excellence and may contextualise the problematic metrics. The exercise of compiling this narrative could be used to open a dialogue about student and teacher university lives, where we acknowledge the common challenges we face (limited time and energy), similarities (commitment to higher learning, disciplinary and institutional affiliation) yet at the same time respect our differences by recognising our complexity (we are so much more than 'student' or 'teacher'), and examine our prejudices. This must be part of a wider project to create, champion and sustain equitable interpersonal-learning relationships and rapport between staff and students.

ACKNOWLEDGEMENTS

This chapter began as student papers presented at the Staff and Educational Development Association's (SEDA) 2017 Spring Conference 'The quest for teaching excellence: issues, resolutions and possibilities'. A conference review considered TEF and unconscious bias (Lawrence, 2017a). We here progress our thinking. We thank SEDA for providing a platform for our original ideas and for ongoing inspiration.

Leanne thanks Ruth Lefever for support and encouragement. Thanks to her guidance Leanne became a PAL Leader as a student, attended the SEDA conference and now contributes to this chapter.

Hollie would like to thank David Cross and Daniel Bown at the University Centre, North Lindsey College, for exemplifying teaching excellence and continuing to encourage and support her throughout her academic journey.

REFERENCES

Ahmed, S. (2017). *Living a feminist life*. Durham, NC: Duke University Press.

Akhtar, A. (2018). The experience of being a student partner in educational development projects. *Educational Developments*, 19(4), 7–8. Retrieved from https://www.seda.ac.uk/past-issues/19.4

Altman, I. (1990). Conceptualizing "rapport". *Psychological Inquiry*, 1(4), 294–297.

Barnet, R. (2014). *Conditions of flexibility: Securing a more responsive higher education system*. York: Higher Education Academy.

Bhopal, K. (2018). *White Privilege: The myth of a post racial society*. Bristol: University of Bristol, Policy Press.

Blackmoore, P, Blackwell, R., & Edmondson, M. (2016). *Tackling wicked issues: Outcomes in the teaching excvellence framework*. Higher Education Policy Institute. Retrieved from https://www.hepi.ac.uk/wp-content/uploads/2016/09/Hepi_TTWI-Web.pdf

Boring, A., Ottoboni, K. & Stark, P. B. (2016). Student evaluations of teaching (mostly) do not measure teaching effectiveness. ScienceOpen Research. Retrieved from https://www.math.upenn.edu/~pemantle/active-papers/Evals/stark2016.pdf

Clapper, T. C. (2015). Cooperative-based learning and the zone of proximal development. *Simulation & Gaming*, 46(2), 148–158.

Criado-Perez, C. (2019). *Invisible women: Exposing data bias in a world designed for men* Chatto & Windus, ISBN 9781784741723.

Equality Challenge Unit. (2013). *Unconscious bias and higher education*. London: ECU.

Feng, S., & Wood, M. (2012). What makes a good university lecturer? Students' perspectives on teaching excellence. *Journal of Applied Research in Higher Education*, 4(2), 142–155.

Flaherty, C. (2019) Teaching evals: Bias and tenure. *Inside Higher Education*. Retrieved from https://www.insidehighered.com/news/2019/05/20/fighting-gender-bias-student-evaluations-teaching-and-tenures-effect-instruction?utm_content=bufferf6f94&utm_medium=social&utm_source=twitter&utm_campaign=IHEbuffer

Freire, P. (2004). *Pedagogy of hope: Reliving pedagogy of the oppressed*. London: Bloomsbury.

Freire, P. (2007). *Pedagogy of the heart*. New York, NY: Continuum.

French, A., & O'Leary, M. (2017). *Teaching excellence in higher education*. Bingley: Emerald Insights. Retrieved from https://www.emerald.com/insight/publication/doi/10.1108/9781787147614

Gordon, N. (2014). *Flexible pedagogies: Technology enhanced learning*. York: Higher Education Academy.

Gunn, V., & Fisk, A. (2013). Considering teaching excellence in higher education 2007–2013. Retrieved from https://tinyurl.com/yc6udssz

Hartley, P. (2017) Teaching Excellence – student perspectives. *Educational Developments* 18(4), pp. 2–3. Retrieved from https://www.seda.ac.uk/past-issues/18.4

Haughton, A., & Anderson, J. (2017). *Embedding mental wellbeing in the curriculum: Maximising success in HE*. York: Higher Education Academy.

hooks, b. (1994). *Teaching to transgress: Education as the practice of freedom*. London: Routledge.

hooks, b. (2003). *Teaching community: A pedagogy of hope*. London: Routledge.

hooks, b. (2010). *Teaching critical thinking: Practical wisdom*. London: Routledge.

Hunt, L. (2017). The importance of rapport in teaching excellence and learning gain. Retrieved from https://www.seda.ac.uk/past-issues/18.4

Lammers, W. J., Gillaspy, J. A., & Hancock, F. (2017). Predicting academic success with early, middle, and late semester assessment of Student–instructor rapport. *Teaching of Psychology*, 44(2), 145–149.

Lawrence, J. (2017a). Reflections on SEDA spring conference *Educational Developments*, 18(3). Retrieved from https://www.seda.ac.uk/past-issues/18.3

Lawrence, J. (2017b). Educator wellbeing and the scholarship of teaching and learning: A virtuous intersection for the learning community. *Educational Developments*, 18(3). Retrieved from https://www.seda.ac.uk/past-issues/18.3

Lawrence, J., & Herrick, T. (2019). Supporting wellbeing through the scholarship of teaching and learning. *Journal of Applied Research in HE*. doi:10.1108/JARHE-

Mathias, L., & Peters, J. (2018). Student-staff partnership in educational development: A source of hope in dark times. *Educational Developments*, 19(4), 4–7. Retrieved from https://www.seda.ac.uk/past-issues/19.4

Mitchell, K., & Martin, J. (2018). Gender bias in student evaluations. *Political Science & Politics*, 51(3), 648–652.

Morrish, L. (2019). *Pressure vessels: The epidemic of poor mental health among higher education staff*. Higher Education Policy Institute. Retrieved from https://www.hepi.ac.uk/2019/05/23/pressure-vessels-the-epidemic-of-poor-mental-health-among-higher-education-staff/

Muneer, R., Cotton, D., & Winter, J. (2015). *7 steps to: Mitigating unconscious bias in teaching and learning*. 7 Steps Series. Educational Development Series. Plymouth: University of Plymouth.

National Union of Students. (2015). *A Manifesto for partnership*. London: NUS. Retrieved from https://www.nusconnect.org.uk/resources/a-manifesto-for-partnership

National Union of Students. (2016, August 10) Open letter TEF is an unreliable test for university teaching. *The Guardian*. Retrieved from https://www.theguardian.com/education/2016/aug/09/tef-is-an-unreliable-test-for-university-teaching

Office for Students. (2019). Participation of local areas in HE. *Office for Students*. Retrieved from https://www.officeforstudents.org.uk/data-and-analysis/polar-participation-of-local-areas/

Reid, L. D. (2010). The role of perceived race and gender in the evaluation of college teaching on RateMyProfessors.com. *National Association of Diversity Officers in Higher Education*, 3(3), 137–152.

Rigby, S. (2017, April). The quest for teaching excellence and learning gain: Issues, resolutions, possibilities. In Staff and educational developers association spring conference, Leeds

Shaw, H. (2017). A widening participation students perspective of teaching excellence in college based higher education. Retrieved from https://www.seda.ac.uk/past-issues/18.4

Smith, B. (2015). The evolution of my rapport: One professor's journey to building successful Instructor/Student relationships. *College Teaching*, 63(2), 35–36.

Starcher, K. (2011). Intentionally building rapport with students. *College Teaching*, 59(4), 162.

Thomas, L. (2012). *Building student engagement and belonging in higher education at a time of change*. York: Advance HE.

University and College Union. (2016). Workload is an education issue: UCU workload report 2016. Retrieved from https://www.ucu.org.uk/media/8195/Workload-is-an-education-issue-UCU-workload-survey-report-2016/pdf/ucu_workloadsurvey_fullreport_jun16.pdf

Wilson, J. H., Ryan, R. G., & Pugh, J. L. (2010). Professor-student rapport scale predicts student outcomes. *Teaching of Psychology*, 37(4), 246.

Wood, P., & O'Leary, M. (2019). Moving beyond teaching excellence: Developing a different narrative for England's higher education sector, *International Journal of Comparative Education and Development*, 21(2), 112–126. doi: 10.1108/IJCED-08-2018-0028

5

'IT'S NOT WHAT GETS TAUGHT, OR HOW WELL IT MAY BE TAUGHT, BUT WHO IS DOING THE TEACHING': CAN STUDENT EVALUATIONS EVER DELIVER A FAIR ASSESSMENT ON TEACHING EXCELLENCE IN HIGHER EDUCATION?

Amanda French

ABSTRACT

This chapter offers a discussion of the increasingly widespread use of student evaluations in higher education. It critiques the extent to which these student evaluations are now regarded by governments and higher education management as an authoritative source of information on all aspects of HE provision, with a particular focus on their use to rank and evaluate teaching excellence through the Teaching Excellence Framework. It provides an overview of research looking into how student perceptions of teachers' teaching

*excellence, or otherwise, play out very differently
depending on the gender, age and social class of the
lecturers doing the teaching. This chapter argues that
these differences make it difficult to ensure that students' assessment of higher education teaching are fair
and/or consistent with regard to the teaching they are
experiencing across different courses, disciplines and
institutions. It concludes that acknowledging how
inequalities will inevitably play a part in any evaluative
processes is a more productive way of thinking about
how more informed indices of teaching quality might be
more usefully understood and operationalised in higher
education. This approach, however, requires HEI's to
recognise the ways in which existing racialised, sexualised and gendered patterns reoccur and sustain
inequalities currently in the UK higher education sector.
(199)*

Keywords: Higher education; student evaluations; staff
discrimination; teaching excellence; HE staff diversity;
HE marketisation

The government's use of the title 'Teaching Excellence
Framework' is deliberate although misleading as none of its
chosen matrixes focus solely on teaching excellence, rather
the title is used to suggest a causal, if disingenuous link
between teaching excellence, student achievement and earning potential. However, this foregrounding of teaching
excellence works because for decades now, UK education
policy has been characterised by Ball's (2003) persuasive
concept of 'performativity' in teaching, which has increasingly required:

> *...the re-invention of [teaching] professionals*
> *themselves as units of resource whose performance*
> *and productivity must constantly be audited so that it*
> *can be enhanced'*

(Shore & Wright, 1999, p. 559).

In order to audit teaching in higher education, a commodified concept of 'student satisfaction' has been operationalised through student evaluations of one type of another which are used in a number of ways in the current global higher education environment (Bolat & O'Sullivan, 2017). For example, in addition to their much vaunted promise to deliver valuable 'big data' to inform and improve provision and facilities for students in universities, national student evaluations, like other education effectiveness matrixes, are increasingly used for commercial purposes, including the ranking of HEIs in various national and international league tables such as the World University Rankings as well as the English Teaching Excellence Framework (TEF) (Gunn, 2018; McCaig, 2018; McGettigan, 2013).

This widespread use of student-generated data signals the extent to which student evaluations are now regarded by governments and higher education management as an authoritative source of information on all aspects of higher education provision (Scullion & Molesworth, 2016; Tomlinson, 2015). Influential national student evaluations of higher education include the UK's National Student Survey (NSS), the American 'National Survey of Student Engagement' and Australia's 'Course Experience Questionnaire'. The use of these national student evaluations in higher education is linked to the increasing attention paid to 'student voice' and 'student experience', especially in the United Kingdom since the introduction of tuition fees. The inexorable growth of national student evaluations is usually justified precisely because, it is claimed, they express the 'student voice' and allow the assessment of the 'student experience'. However, how one defines, especially at a national level, a meaningful 'student voice' (Robinson & Taylor, 2013) and how the 'student experience' (Sabri, 2011) can be evaluated is problematic and highly contested.

The ubiquity of national student evaluations reflects a tight policy focus on student engagement and outcomes expressed through a concomitant commodification and veneration of student feedback by governments and university management. A manifestation of the Global Education Reform Movement (GERM), student evaluations are driven by its three main policy principles: accountability, standards and decentralisation. Indeed, it is easy to track how over the last 30 years, in England and Wales particularly, educational data mining in HEIs has been increasingly influenced by countless GERM accountability and measurement policy initiatives, culminating to date in the TEF, a key plank of the 2017 Higher Education Reform Act (HERA) (O'Leary & French, 2017). Of interest to the focus of this chapter is the fact that the NSS is one of the only sources of data that touches specifically on teaching excellence in the TEF. Despite their much debated shortcomings, the material generated from the NSS and in-house student feedback is currently used to inform not only internal quality processes but contributes to the 'additional contextual information' provided by HEIs as part of an institution's TEF submission. (They will also be one of the primary sources of information for the forthcoming subject-based TEFs.)

As in any neoliberal model of education, TEF positions higher education students as consumers. Consequently, their opinion of the 'product' they have been 'sold', namely their degree, and the people responsible for delivering it 'at the chalk face', their teachers, require careful scrutiny (by government, by parents and by students themselves) in order that they can be judged to see if they and it have been 'value for money' (VFM) (Naidoo, Shankar, & Veer, 2011). While the TEF has only been in place since 2017, it is clear that the UK government is interested to see the extent to which prospective students already regard TEF ratings positively or negatively, and if those ratings might influence their choice of HEI. The survey carried out annually by the Universities and Colleges Admissions service (UCAS) for prospective students included for the first time in 2018 a number of questions about the TEF. Out of the half a million applicants who had applied by the 15 January deadline, 85,000 responded to the new TEF questions, a response rate of approximately 15%. Out of that number, 17.1% stated that they 'had heard of the TEF' prior to making their applications before UCAS's January deadline. 58% of that group stated that the TEF awards were 'important' or 'extremely important' when deciding which HEI to apply to, and that they were more likely to apply to an institution with a TEF Gold rating. Meanwhile, three out of every five respondents who did not know what the TEF was said they would have found the awards 'important', or 'extremely important', had they known about them.

This suggests as more potential students become aware of the TEF, even in its current form as a rather vaguely defined proxy for teaching quality, that it will function in exactly the way that Government hoped it would, as a market indicator. It is perhaps, however, predictable that the UCAS report makes no attempt to find out if those potential applicants who had heard of the TEF actually knew anything about how it had been put together or how the ratings had been achieved. A proxy, after all, works because it does not invite or require close scrutiny of itself, rather it stands for/stands in for something else, usually in order for the 'something else' to be measured or compared. In its survey, the TEF was clearly being positioned unproblematically by UCAS as a proxy for assessing the quality of teaching prospective students can expect to receive at any given HEI.

Students, in addition to the NSS described above, are also exhorted throughout their time at university to complete endless in-house pre-module, mid-module evaluations and overall course evaluations. A recent UCU report exploring the impact and implications of the TEF for lecturers in UK HEIs (O'Leary, Cui, & French, 2019) reported that a significant number of teaching staff in UK HEIs had experienced an increase in what they called 'monitoring mechanisms and accountability procedures' linked to student feedback of one kind or another since the implementation of the TEF (although they did not always directly link them to the TEF). These included an increase in standardised in-house module and programme evaluations, which undoubtedly facilitated a corresponding rise in the use of learning analytics to assess provision. In-house module evaluations in UK universities, like their US equivalents, Student Evaluations of Teaching (SETs), are rather blunt instruments that do little to capture the complexity of teaching and learning interactions. They are usually designed to elicit quantitative and qualitative information, the former usually through a 1–5 Likert scale or multiple choice questions, supplemented by student comments through an open-text boxes, which provides the latter.

Despite their limitations, all student evaluations, to a greater or lesser extent, are invested with a rather specious authority which endows the 'student voice' about the 'student experience' with authenticity, validity and reliability, even though they are arguably, for reasons I go on to discuss below, quite suspect. Indeed, the fragility of their assumed authority is reflected in the extent to which most contemporary research on student evaluation focusses on the need to improve student survey design methods (Richardson, 2005; Sulis, Porcu, & Capursi, 2019) rather than any discussion of what they actually reveal. Nonetheless, the assumption of a 'scientific' or empirical veneer for student evaluations, both national and in-house, is necessary because they are so frequently mobilised by senior HEI management and governments, not only to justify specific internal strategic plans and processes (for example, promotion, redundancy and the development or running down of different departments) but to respond to broad policy edicts like the TEF.

In addition to the difficulties in actually measuring the quality of teaching discussed elsewhere in this collection, there is a body of research exploring how student perceptions of teachers' teaching excellence, or otherwise, in higher education play out very differently depending on variables such as the gender, age and social class of the lecturers doing the teaching. This chapter argues that student responses to these differences make it difficult to ensure that their assessment of the higher education teaching they receive is fair and/or consistent. In particular, this question of fairness and consistency in student evaluations has implications for teaching staff in higher education who deviate from the ste-reotype of the white, straight, middle-class male university lecturer. Indeed, it appears likely that student assumptions and prejudices about gender, race, disability and sexuality, expressed through their evaluation of the teaching they receive in higher education, can constitute a form of discrimination facing many lecturers.

Moreover this is a form of discrimination which largely goes unrecognised but is extremely potentially damaging when such evaluations are mobilised for evaluative purposes, as they are in the TEF, as the NSS is one of the matrixes used in the formulation of the TEF rating for each English HEI.

There is a precedent for this claim as many studies in the United States have shown that SETS reflect student bias against black and female lecturers (Abrami, d'Apollonia, & Rosenfield, 2007; Benton & Cashin, 2014). Unfortunately, very little work has been done to see if the same could be said about national and in-house evaluations in UK HEIs. However, the consequences for individual lecturers of a failure to score well on student evaluations of their teaching quality remain high.

In the light of these concerns, this chapter, therefore, seeks to critically interrogate the rather doubtful claims often made about student evaluations. In particular, it challenges the claim that they are a reliable arbiter of 'value for money' (VFM) in higher education. It does so on the grounds that student evaluations of teaching are essentially experiential and subjective, something which rarely gets acknowledged even when research has explored the extent to which they are affected by other factors including the gender or race of the lecturer (Benton & Cashin, 2014; Darwin, 2016; Richardson, 2005). This is not to say that student-generated data could not be harnessed more effectively to engage students in meaningful dialogue about the quality of their various experiences in higher education (something that will be explored in the final section of this chapter). However, Tomlinson's (2015) study into student perceptions of themselves as consumers highlights how most HEIs currently fail to understand how, in a highly marketised higher education sector, they actually make sense of students' complex relationships with their university and the staff, professional and academic, who work there. Moreover, there is evidence to suggest, that in line with wider neoliberal conceptions of individualism, competition and the VFM agenda in higher education, that HEI's have been more inclined to cast students in the role of informed consumers of a 'university experience', who have exercised rational choice over the private investment they have made in their own education by signing up for a degree. This, of course, is arguably more straightforward than asking them to grapple with the complexities of effective teaching and learning, the vagaries of the labour market for graduate employment across different disciplines and the inherent inequalities of the higher education sector in its current hierarchised form.

Meanwhile students, via these various surveys and evaluations, have endless opportunities to award plaudits or express disappointment on everything they experience whilst at university, from the price and availability of the parking on campus and the quality of the food in the canteens to how well they feel they have been prepared for the world of work and taught their subject. A corollary of the 'the customer knows best' ethos, this aspect of marketisation in HE encourages the illusion of a kind of democratisation of accountability to students-as-customers (perhaps best encapsulated by the vacuous sloganeering of, '*you said, we did*'). However, whilst accepting that student surveys can usefully highlight levels of student discontent regarding, say, the library's inadequate resources or poorly ventilated classrooms, the legitimacy of students' perceptions about the quality of teaching they experience in HE should be treated with caution. This is because student evaluations about the quality and efficacy of the teaching they received whilst at university, as opposed to the question of whether they liked or disliked their tutors or enjoyed some teaching sessions more than others, are inherently problematic. To take them seriously in their current form, as a way of understanding how to improve higher education teaching assumes, with very little empirical evidence, that students possess a critical understanding of how and why they are taught in certain ways (Nast, 1999). Moreover, students' conceptions about teaching are essentially subjective, which, to be fair, is not surprising as they can only be based on individuals' usually limited experience of higher education teaching (after all most of them pass through HE only once as undergraduates).

Packaging student voice and experience through neatly delineated educational effectiveness evaluations like the NSS clearly belies the actual complexity involved in teaching and learning interactions. As Wood (2017) states

> ...*teaching [is] emergent, multifaceted and contextually based. It refutes notions of 'best practice' and argues that any attempt to capture 'excellent practice' is to reduce the holistic nature of the processes that bring teaching, learning, curriculum and assessment together.*

(pg. 40)

As suggested above, however, it appears that governments find it easier to rely on often superficial student evaluations of teaching rather than spend time and money exploring it with teachers and students given that identifying and measuring indices of teaching excellence or quality are so notoriously difficult to determine (O'Leary & Wood, 2019). Nor do they acknowledge or explore any wider social and cultural factors that might affect students' perceptions of teaching including racism, sexism and homophobia, issues that are explored in the next section of this chapter. For these reasons it can be argued that if such perceptions remain unexamined, the credence given to students' evaluation of their teaching in higher education by government and management will inevitably have unpredictable and unfair consequences for many HE staff engaged in teaching.

For example, a number of US studies have revealed that low scores in student evaluations can be used to initiate disciplinary action against higher education teachers often affecting any future chances of promotion (Centra &

Gaubatz, 2000; Davis, 2009; Young, Rush, & Shaw, 2009). Hornstein (2017) makes the important point that although SETs were intended, when first introduced in the 1970s, to be developmental and help improve the quality of teaching, they have subsequently become the dominant indicator of teacher competence in US higher education, often used to help decide promotions and tenure. A recent report in the United Kingdom, commissioned by the Union for Colleges and Universities (UCU) in (2018) *Understanding, recognising and rewarding teaching quality in higher education: an exploration of the impact and implications of the Teaching Excellence Framework* (O'Leary, Cui and French), was the first to explore the views of large numbers of staff working in HEIs about the TEF and its focus on teaching excellence. Unfortunately, many of its respondents reported similar punitive responses by management to low NSS and in-house student evaluations, such as courses being put into 'special measures' which included staff being given targets to achieve higher NSS scores next time round. This kind of knee-jerk response to poor student evaluations, if allowed to go unchallenged, conjures up dystopian image of a performativity/audit culture where higher education teaching staff are principally viewed as units of resource whose academic labour is only measured in terms of the economic needs of their employers (How much do you cost to employ? How many students can you teach?) and their customers, the students (What am I paying for and am I getting my money's worth?).

All of which is not to say that it is not important for HEIs to monitor and quality assure their teaching provision. Issues like the transparency and consistency of assessment processes, the relevance and currency of curriculum content and efficacy and accessibility of teachers are live issues. Teaching staff and students should be able to comment on and ultimately inform policy and practice around them. However, as discussed above, because tuition fees position students as consumers, universities have an unsurprising tendency to frame student dissatisfaction with teaching as a 'customer satisfaction issue' rather than an opportunity to discuss pedagogic processes and practice. This has resulted in a common institutional nervousness about managing student complaints about assessment, curriculum and teaching, especially when they are couched in terms of the students asserting that they did not get the grade they 'wanted' or 'expected' or 'had paid for'. Despite the well-researched complexity of teaching and learning interactions and their often uncertain correlation to learning outcomes, there is a simplistic propensity for poor grades to be blamed on poor teaching students and management.

Such a narrow VFM agenda can easily end up treating teaching staff as if they were all the same sort of widgets whose continued employment relies on successfully meeting a series of allegedly neutral performance indicators. These indicators include the percentage of their students achieving 'good' degrees and their rates of pay 5 years after they graduate, (both TEF benchmarks) as well as high marks in student evaluations which rate them on overtly subjective questions like 'Staff are good at explaining things' and 'Staff have made the subject interesting' (both NSS questions). Such a working environment, hedged about, as it so often is, with short-term fixed contracts and performance-related pay, encourages compliance and reduces the willingness of teaching staff in higher education to challenge negative comments about their management of students and/or their delivery of their subject. Over time, therefore student evaluations, like other education effectiveness matrixes, increasingly have the potential to be used by management as tools to insist on more centralised control of teaching processes and practices. This can and has resulted in the forced removal of unpopular programmes, assessment models and delivery styles as well as the marginalisation of noncompliant teaching staff; all of which ultimately limits academic freedom and professional auton- omy within the higher education sector. Simultaneously, such centralised control inhibits the development of innovative and creative learning which has to be to the detriment of students, irrespective of their discipline.

In antithesis to the VFM agenda, this chapter argues that an evaluation of the quality of teaching and the learning experience that it produces are mutually constituted through the relationship between the lecturer and the student(s) involved. However, the idea that all such teaching and learning relationships are equally constituted in the same way (and can be evaluated/understood using the same instrument of measurement) is problematic. In order to begin to rethink it, one can evoke Stuart Hall's (1997) 'articulation of certain kinds of differences' to account for how any mutual consti- tution of the quality of teaching and learning will inevitably be mediated by certain kinds of inequalities. Acknowledging, therefore, that difference and inequalities will inevitably play a part in any evaluative process is a more productive way of thinking about how more informed indices of teaching quality might be usefully understood and operationalised in higher education. This approach, however, requires an exploration of how existing racialised, sexualised and gendered patterns reoccur and sustain inequalities currently in the UK higher education sector.

To try and frame its critical interrogation of student eval- uations, this chapter prefers to view higher education teaching staff as 'embodied subjects' (Shilling, 2005) working in highly contested political spaces where they are positioned in distinct ways as providers of teaching to students. Examples of research that help explore how and why students evaluations discriminate against certain groups of teaching staff in higher education will be explored and discussed, in the next section, using the concept of intersectionality as an overarching theory in recognition of the disadvantage created by membership of other groups in society including disability, LGBTQ+, age or religion. Crenshaw (1989) initially coined the term 'intersectionality' using it to challenge the tendency to 'treat race and gender as mutually exclusive categories of experience and analysis'. Hill Collins usefully operationalises the term as follows:

> *As a heuristic device … [that] references the ability of social phenomena such as race, class, and gender to mutually construct one another. One can use the framework of intersectionality to think through social institutions, organizational structures, patterns of social interactions and other social practices on all levels of social organization'*

(Hill-Collins, 1998, p. 205).

Intersectionality is a useful concept because it insists on examining how location (time and space) works together with personal factors like race, class and sexuality and gender, to constitute lecturers as embodied subjects differently and inequitably within higher education. This intersectional approach to how and why students perceive and judge higher education teaching staff differently acknowledges that there is more than one type of disadvantage – and advantage – which exist, often simultaneously.

In this way, intersectionality helps to explore how lecturers and students are all always colocated in multiple ways within instances of teaching and learning allowing for critical interrogation of how student-generated data play out differently for different higher education lecturers. Specifically, it helps identity how the different personal categories to which higher education lecturers belong reflect the different power

relations that characterise their teaching and learning interactions. This means that teaching staff and students are never
located in a singular power position defined by each other's
race, gender, sexuality, disability, etc. This chapter will
therefore draw on feminist (Ahmed, 2004, 2007) and Critical
Race Theory (Delgado & Stefancic, 2001), along with queer
and disabled critical concepts of exclusion and othering to
interrogate the values and processes underpinning educational effectiveness' matrixes based on student evaluations. In
doing so, it points to a way to possibly rehabilitate student
evaluations through deconstructing and challenging the
normative and discriminatory values that they often reveal
but do not acknowledge.

In the United States, there is plenty of evidence to suggest
that students' evaluation of the teaching they experience in
higher education is more likely to reflect their biases, prejudices towards those that teach them (Abrami et al., 2007;
Benton & Cashin, 2014; Nast, 1999), as well as any mis-
conceptions about teaching per se that they may harbour
(Steward & Phelps, 2000). For example, there is a tradition
of research going back several decades that suggests that US
higher education students perceive, evaluate and treat female
lecturers quite differently than they do their male counterparts. This suggests that student evaluations persistently
reproduce gendered responses which reflect wider social and
cultural sexual stereotyping, rather than informed responses
to their teaching and learning experiences (Basow, 1995;
Centra & Gaubatz, 2000; Feldman, 1992; Young, Rush, &
Shaw, 2009). Research conducted at the University of California, for example, found that female staff consistently
received lower scores on student evaluations of teaching
(Boring, Ottoboni, & Stark, 2016). Likewise, a study in
Canada found that female tutors were more likely to be
judged harshly than male tutors in student evaluations when

they did not give higher marks. Indeed, students receiving lower marks often made reference to negative female gender stereotypes with regard to the female teachers who had marked their work (Sinclair & Zunda 2000).

While a general consensus exists that gender plays a role in how students perceive and interact with their lecturers, it is difficult to work out how this is also affected by variations in several mediating factors including disciplinary fields, teaching styles and subject material. It is inevitably problematic to isolate gender as a source for student bias after face to face teaching as there are so many other variations that might affect a student's perception of the learning experience. However, MacNell, Driscoll, and Hunt's (2015) USA study created two assistant instructors in an online class who each operated under two different gender identities. In their evaluations, students consistently rated the assumed male instructor significantly more positively than the assumed female counterpart. Interestingly, the degree of gender bias evinced by the students varied depending on other factors such as student's gender, their age and the area and discipline they were working in, factors that in themselves warrant further investigation as they too could be gendered or affected by other variables. The study also revealed the effect of gender of student evaluations of teaching is also apparent in the choice of language deployed in responses to open-text questions by students in teaching evaluations. For example, in MacNell et al. (2015), students described the 'male' online instructor as *'brilliant, awesome and knowledgeable'*, but when the same teaching experience was thought to come from a woman, 'she' was categorised as *'bossy and annoying'*.

Studies focussing on the reactions of students to black teaching staff in higher education have found similar prejudices surfacing. Recent research conducted in the United Kingdom

(Bell & Brooks, 2016) found that by cross-referencing NSS scores with statistics on staff demographics from the Higher Education Statistics Agency (HESA), they could show that the ethnicity of lecturers had a significant impact on NSS scores, with black, Asian and minority ethnic (BAME) lecturers consistently being scored lower than their white counterparts. This work echoed research in the United States, which found that black and minority ethnic teachers tended to be evaluated more harshly on websites like RateMyProfessor.com (Close Subtirelu, 2015). The chapter 'Rapport and Relationships: The Student Perspective on Teaching Excellence' (Lawrence, Hunt, Shaw and Synmioe) in this collection also raises the question of how different groups of students, in this instance, those with a widening participation profile may have different expectations and assumptions about teaching, which again are not acknowledged in current student evaluations.

Ahmed (2004) has argued that academic authority does not seem to 'stick' to female or black academics in the same way as it does to their white counterparts, rendering them at a distinct disadvantage when it comes to asking students to measure their quality and effectiveness as higher education lecturers through matrixes like NSS which then contribute to institutional TEF ratings. Judgements about what a higher education lecturer's look like, sound like, act like can be linked to prejudices that students may harbour without fully understanding why as they are so deeply ingrained. As Puwar (2004) notes:

> [...] some bodies through their history are seen as natural occupants of specific spaces, some bodies have the right to belong in certain locations, while others are marked out as trespasser's, and therefore out of place.

> (p.51).

Trotman (2009) examines the impact of what she calls the 'imposter phenomenon' to describe how black women have been doubly victimised by scholarly neglect and racist assumptions which often leaves them feeling exposed and vulnerable in higher education. Similarly, Leach (2007) succinctly terms the position of lesbian, gay bisexual and transgender workers as 'space invaders', which perhaps goes some way to explaining why students often view them and their academic labour in more negative terms than their white and heterosexual colleagues. One also needs to take into consideration how lecturers who do not fit the norm feel themselves about their vulnerable position in higher education. Research by Wright, Thompson and Channer (2007) focuses on British universities and examines the experiences and challenges faced by Black women in academia, which often centre around their acute awareness that they occupy a space traditionally reserved for their white middle-class counterparts. Finally, Rollock (2019), Alexander and Arday (2015) and Bhopal (2016) have all done more recent valuable research on how UK BAME academics have consistently been subject to racial discrimination and increased precarity in higher education by management.

In the light of the above research findings, not surprisingly perhaps, many staff in higher education are increasingly fearful of student evaluations, especially as the TEF encourages such an unhelpful focus on the 'performance of teaching' (Ball, 2012) rather than any meaningful understanding of the quality of the teaching and learning interactions that students are experiencing with different teachers. As Ball writes:

> [...]Within the rigours and disciplines of
> performativity we are required to spend increasing
> amounts of our time in making ourselves
> accountable, reporting on what we do rather than

> *doing it. There are new sets of skills to be acquired*
> *here: skills of presentation and of inflation, making*
> *the most of ourselves, making a spectacle of*
> *ourselves.*

(2012, 30)

These skills of 'presentation' which involve enacting a performance of excellent teaching are clearly more difficult to achieve when the 'actors' enacting them do not, as discussed previously, 'look the part' to begin with. Without being willing to critically investigate the different ways in which different groups of staff across higher education are perceived, the government and management are missing important information on how students' evaluation of their experience of teaching in higher education plays out perversely for some groups of lecturers, and more importantly how those evaluations can be productively challenged.

This chapter does not seek to reject the usefulness of student evaluations in any circumstances, rather it is asking for a more nuanced approach to their use, both in terms of how they are designed and how they are used to inform policy and practice in higher education. In the first instance, there is a case for saying that universities need to invest more time in informing and preparing students to make meaningful and informed valuations. Currently there is no evidence to show that HEIs are working to help students think critically about what constitutes teaching quality and effectiveness, prior to being asked to judge their lecturers.

Additionally, universities need to acknowledge the impact that the lack of staff diversity has on students' judgements. Until the last century, women, BAME, disabled and LTBG + people have politically, historically and socially been excluded and marginalised both within and outside of the traditionally very privileged space that universities occupy in English society. There also needs to be active consideration, and more importantly, more research into how students' own educational background, as well as gender and ethnicity, could affect their perceptions and judgement on lecturers' teaching. Such research could form part of TEF's 'lessons learned exercise' as refinements to the process are made for future years. In short, there is an opportunity to develop a TEF that addresses the implications of potentially 'othered' staff identities for staff as well as students.

In conclusion, this chapter has argued that the TEF's use of both national and in-house evaluative data from students needs to be more attuned to the limitations and shortcomings of student evaluations as a way of measuring and comparing 'teaching excellence'. It has argued for a more nuanced understanding of how students experience their teaching and learning interactions with lecturers. One that is fluid and allows for complexity and a recognition that teaching and learning is necessarily experienced very differently across the very diverse institutions disciplines and courses that characterise higher education provision. These differences moreover need, if they are to be meaningful, to be judged on their own terms, as well as in relation to similar forms of provision. In particular, there needs to be a sector-wide commitment to challenging the extent to which, as the research cited in this chapter suggests, student conceptualisations of teaching quality are often unconsciously and consciously reproducing entrenched white/male/heteronormative/able-bodied lecturer archetypes which create a powerful lens through which teaching competence and confidence are viewed.

Likewise, the wider social impacts of homophobia, disablism sexism and racism need to be acknowledged at a structural, institutional level in higher education, with staff and students, as part of their everyday teaching and learning interactions. However, although diversity initiatives can reveal 'the gap between words, images and deeds' (Ahmed, 2007, p. 607), there is a need to ensure that they lead to action (Pilkington, 2013). For example, there could be a commitment by Government to experiment with more sophisticated, sensitive evaluative instruments and institutional strategies that could help critique and explore the diversity of learning processes and pedagogic approaches in contemporary higher education and which recognise the centrality and complexity of the emotions and practical skills involved in learning and teaching. This goes beyond a commitment from managers to support all staff who take curricular and pedagogical risks, but to also recognise that some staff are more vulnerable and/or precariously positioned within the Academy, irrespective of how they teach.

The current focus in the TEF on increasingly standardised performance outputs, often far removed from the demands of everyday teaching for teaching staff, does nothing to encourage a productive or positive climate of cooperation and collaboration around teaching and teaching development. Instead, to date, the TEF appears to have further legitimised an already established tendency by the executive in higher education towards micromanagement and endless target setting. Furthermore, set against a higher education environment beset with threats about reduced provision, cuts in funding and resultant employment insecurity, teaching staff feel under pressure to meet targets and comply with institutional edicts around curriculum and assessment. Consequently, as Holley, Sinfield, and Burns (2006) found in their research about widening participation students:

> . . . [lecturer] strategies for responding to students are
> not governed by student need – but by management

172 Amanda French

and government targets – and in the end, the students
are further unsupported and silenced.

(Holley et al., 2006, p. 4)

This then is the final reason that we need to rethink student evaluations and, in particular, the role they play in the TEF and in-house institutional policy-making. It is that it is questionable that they actually, in their current form, do allow for the actual variety of student opinions about the teaching that they receive in higher education, both negative and positive, to be heard and acted on in any meaningful way. By engaging in a more multifaceted, nuanced dialogue with students teaching staff will be more able to share and explore existing effective teaching practices and develop new more inclusive and creative ways of learning in higher education. Essentially, actions speak louder than words and until new approaches to student evaluations become part of a comprehensive strategy for equality, diversity and inclusivity owned and driven by policy-makers and senior managers across higher education nothing will change.

REFERENCES

Abrami, P. C., d'Apollonia, S., & Rosenfield, S. (2007). The dimensionality of student ratings of instruction: What we know and what we do not. In R. P. Perry & J. C. Smart (Eds.), *The scholarship of teaching and learning in higher education: An evidence-based perspective* (pp. 385–445). Dordrecht: Springer.

Ahmed, S. (2004). *The cultural politics of emotion*. Edinburgh: Edinburgh University Press.

Ahmed, S. (2007). A phenomenology of whiteness. *Feminist Theory*, *8*(2), 149–168.

Alexander, C., & Arday, J. (Eds.). (2015). *Aiming higher: Race, inequality and diversity in the academy*, London: Runnymede.

Ball, S. (2003). The teacher's soul and the terrors of performativity. *Journal of Education Policy*, *18*(2), 215–228.

Ball, S. J. (2012). The making of a neoliberal academic. *Research in secondary teacher education*, *2*(1), 29–31.

Basow, S. A. (1995). Student evaluations of college professors: When gender matters. *Journal of Educational Psychology*, *87*, 656–665.

Bell, A., & Brooks, C. (2016, June). Is there a magic link between research activity, professional teaching qualifications and student satisfaction? Social Science Research Network. Retrieved from http://ssrn.com/abstract=2712 412. Accessed on December 12, 2019.

Benton, S. L., & Cashin, W. E. (2014). Student ratings of instruction in college and university courses. In M. B. Paulsen (Ed.), *Higher education: Handbook of theory & research* (29, pp. 279–326). Dordrecht: Springer.

Bhopal, K. (2016). *The experiences of black and minority ethnic academics: A comparative study of the unequal academy*. London; New York, NY: Routledge.

Bolat, E., & O'Sullivan, H. (2017). Radicalising the marketing of higher education: Learning from student-generated social media data. *Journal of Marketing Management*, *33*(9–10), 742–763.

Boring, A., Ottoboni, K., & Stark, P. B. (2016). Student evaluations of teaching (mostly) do not measure teaching effectiveness. ScienceOpen Research, 7 January 2016.

Retrieved from https://www.scienceopen.com/document?
vid=818d8ec0-5908-47d8-86b4-5dc38f04b23e. Accessed
on November 16, 2019.

Centra, J. A., & Gaubatz, N. B. (2000). Is there gender bias in
student evaluations of teaching? *Journal of Higher Education, 71*, 17–33.

Close Subtirelu, N. (2015). "She does have an accent but…":
Race and language ideology in students' evaluations of
mathematics instructors on RateMyProfessors.com.
Language in Society, 44(1), 35–62.

Crenshaw, K. (1989). Demarginalizing the intersection of race
and sex: A black feminist critique of antidiscrimination
doctrine, feminist theory and antiracist politics. University
of Chicago Legal Forum (pp. 139–167).

Darwin, S. (2016). The emergence of contesting motives for
student feedback-based evaluation in Australian higher
education. *Higher Education Research and Development,
35*(3), 419–432.

Davis, B. G. (2009). *Tools for teaching (2nd ed.)*. San Fran-
cisco, CA: John Wiley & Sons.

Delgado, R., & Stefancic, J. (2001). *Critical race theory: An
introduction*. New York, NY: New York University Press.

Feldman, K. A. (1992). College students' views of male and
female college teachers: Evidence from the social labora-
tory and experiments – Part 1. *Research in Higher Education, 33*, 317–375.

Gunn, A. (2018). Metrics and methodologies for measuring
teaching quality in higher education: Developing the
Teaching Excellence Framework (TEF). *Educational
Review, 70*(2), 129–148. doi:10.1080/00131911.2017.
1410106

Hall, S. (1997). *Representation: Cultural representations and signifying practices*. London: SAGE Publications.

Hill-Collins, P. (1998). *Fighting words: Black women and the search for justice*. Minneapolis, MN: University of Minnesota Press.

Holley, D., Sinfield, S., & Burns, T. (2006). "It was horrid, very very horrid": A student perspective on coming to an inner city university in the UK. *Social Responsibility Journal*, 2(1), 36–41.

Hornstein, H. (2017). Student evaluations of teaching are an inadequate assessment tool for evaluating faculty performance. *Cogent Education*, 4(1) (published online). Retrieved from https://www.tandfonline.com/doi/full/10.1080/233118 6X.2017.1304016 Accessed on January, 2020.

Leach, T. (2007). Space invaders: Race, gender and bodies out of place. *Equal Opportunities International*, 26(5), 507–514.

MacNell, L., Driscoll, A., & Hunt, A. N. (2015). 'What's in a name': Exposing gender bias in student ratings of teaching. *Innovative Higher Education*, 40(4), 291–303.

McCaig, C. (Ed.). (2018). Continuity and discontinuity on the road to risk and exit: Stages of marketisation in comparative policy analysis. In *The marketisation of English higher education (great debates in higher education)*. Bingley: Emerald Publishing Limited.

McGettigan, A. (2013). *The Great University Gamble: Money, markets and the future of higher education*. London: Pluto Press.

Naidoo, R., Shankar, A., & Veer, E. (2011). The consumerist turn in higher education: Policy aspirations and outcomes. *Journal of marketing management*, 27(11–12), 1142–1162.

Nast, H. (1999). 'Sex', 'Race' and Multiculturalism: Critical consumption and the politics of course evaluations. *Journal of Geography in Higher Education*, *23*(1), 102–115.

O'Leary, M., & Wood, P. (2017). The failings of marketised measurement in capturing the complexity of teaching and learning: the case of lesson observation in the English Further Education sector. *Professional Development in Education*, *43*(4), 573–591.

O'Leary, M., Cui, V., & French, A. (2019). Understanding, recognising and rewarding teaching quality in higher education: An exploration of the impact and implications of the teaching excellence framework. University and Colleges Union, Birmingham. Retrieved from https://www.ucu.org.uk/media/10092/Impact-of-TEF-report-Feb-2019/pdf/Impactof TEFreportFEb2019. Accessed on July 2019.

O'Leary, M., & French, A. (2017). *Excellence in higher education, challenges, changes and the teaching excellence framework*. Bingley: Emerald Publishing Limited.

Pilkington, A. (2013). The interacting dynamics of institutional racism in higher education. *Race, Ethnicity and Education*, *16*(2), 225–245.

Puwar, N. (2004). *Space invaders race, gender and bodies out of place*. Oxford: Berg Publishers.

Richardson, J. T. E. (2005). Instruments for obtaining student feedback: A review of the literature. *Assessment & Evaluation in Higher Education*, *30*(4), 387–415.

Robinson, C., & Taylor, C. (2013). Student voice as a contested practice: Power and participation in two student voice projects. *Improving Schools*, *16*(1), 32–46.

Rollock, N. (2019). *Staying power: The career experiences and strategies of UK black female professors*. Project Report. UCU, London. Accessed January 2020 https://www.ucu.org.uk/media/10075/staying-power/pdf/ucu_rollock_february_2019.pdf

Sabri, D. (2011). What's wrong with 'the student experience'? *Discourse: Studies in the Cultural Politics of Education*, 32(5), 657–667.

Scullion, R., & Molesworth, M. (2016). Normalisation of and resistance to consumer behaviour in higher education. *Journal of Marketing for Higher Education*, 26(2), 129–131.

Shilling, C. (2005). *The body in culture, technology and society*. London; Thousand Oaks, CA; New Delhi: SAGE Publications.

Shore, C., & Wright, S. (1999). Audit culture and anthropology: Neo-liberalism in British higher education. *The Journal of the Royal Anthropological Institute*, 5(4), 557–575.

Sinclair, L., & Zunda, K. (2000). Motivated stereotyping of women: she's fine if she praised me but incompetent if she criticised me. *Personality and Social Psychology Bulletin*, 26(11), 1329–1342.

Steward, R. J., & Phelps, R. E. (2000). Faculty of color and university students: Rethinking the evaluation of faculty teaching. *Journal of the Research Association of Minority Professors*, 4, 49–56.

Sulis, I., Porcu, M., & Capursi, V. (2019). On the use of student evaluation of teaching: A longitudinal analysis combining measurement issues and implications of the exercise. *Social Indicators Research*, 142(3), 1305–1331.

Tomlinson, M. (2015). Student perceptions of themselves as 'consumers' of higher education. *British Journal of Sociology of Education*, *38*(4), 1–15.

Trotman, F. K. (2009). The imposter phenomenon among african american women in the U.S. institutions of higher education: Implications for counseling. Compelling Counseling. Interventions. Retrieved from http://counselingoutfitters.com/vistas/vistas09/Article_8_Trotman.pdf. Accessed on December 2019.

Wood, P. (2017). From teaching excellence to emergent pedagogies: A complex process alternative to understanding the role of teaching in higher education. In A. French & M. O'Leary (Eds.), *Teaching excellence in higher education: Challenges, changes and the teaching excellence framework* (pp. 39–74). Bingley: Emerald Publishing Limited.

Wright, C., Thompson, S., & Channer, Y. (2007). Out of Place: Black women academics in British universities. *Women's History Review*, *16*(2), 145–162.

Young, S., Rush, L., & Shaw, D. (2009). Evaluating gender bias in ratings of university instructors' teaching effectiveness. *International Journal for the Scholarship of Teaching & Learning*, *3*, 1–14.

6

QUEERING THE TEF

Brendan Bartram

ABSTRACT

Taken at face value, it may initially seem difficult to argue with the sentiments enshrined in the rhetoric that surrounds the TEF – raising the status of teaching in Higher Education (HE), rebalancing its relationship with research, incentivising institutions to focus on the quality of teaching and making them more accountable for 'how well they ensure excellent outcomes for their students in terms of graduate-level employment or further study' (OfS, 2018, p. 1). Clearly, these are laudable aspirations that will chime with anyone who believes in the importance of students experiencing an education that enriches and transforms them and their potential. Drawing on Fraser and Lamble's (2014/2015) use of queer theory in relation to pedagogy, however, this chapter aims to expose the TEF not just 'as a landmark initiative that is designed to further embed a neoliberal audit and monitoring culture into Higher Education' (Rudd, 2017, p. 59) but as a constraining exercise that restrains diversity and limits potential. Although queer theory is

more usually linked with gender and sexuality studies,
Fraser and Lamble show us that it can be used 'in its
broader political project of questioning norms, opening
desires and creating possibilities' (p. 64). In this way, the
queer theoretical lens used here helps us to question,
disrupt and contest the essentialising hegemonic logics
behind the nature and purposes of the TEF and its effects
in HE classrooms. Using the slantwise position of the
homosexual (Foucault, 1996), this queer analysis of the
TEF can thus be helpful as a politically generative exer-
cise in opening up space for new possibilities.

Keywords: Teaching excellence; queer theory;
neoliberalism; TEF; higher education; consumerism

INTRODUCTION

Taken at face value, it would seem difficult to argue with the
sentiments enshrined in the rhetoric that surrounds the TEF –
raising the status of teaching in Higher Education (HE), rebalancing its relationship with research, incentivising institutions
to focus on the quality of teaching and making them more
accountable for 'how well they ensure excellent outcomes for
their students in terms of graduate-level employment or further
study' (OfS, 2018, p. 1). Clearly, language such as this speaks
to laudable aspirations that will chime with anyone who
believes in the importance of students experiencing an education that enriches them and enhances their potential. This
impression of educational respectability may not be quite what
it seems, however. The aim of this chapter is to peer below this
veneer to reveal a rather different perspective on the TEF. To
do this, it draws on queer theory to expose the TEF not just 'as
a landmark initiative that is designed to further embed a
neoliberal audit and monitoring culture into Higher Education'

(Rudd, 2017, p. 59) but as a constraining exercise that restrains diversity and limits potential. The chapter begins with a brief discussion of queer theory, before moving on to an examination of the TEF's central features. This is followed by a review of the ways in which the TEF operates to sustain a narrow student identity rather than enable more diverse constructions and possibilities. It then explores the effects of propagating this singular identity before returning to queer theory to consider more optimistic possibilities.

QUEER THEORY?

The decision to use queer theory as a vehicle for critiquing the TEF might initially seem an unusual manoeuvre. This section therefore aims to explore briefly the nature of this academic field in an attempt to examine how it can be used to challenge the TEF's operationalisation and logics. Providing a widely agreed definition of queer theory is far from straightforward, and many scholars have noted the slipperiness of attempts to define the discipline and delineate its parameters (Sullivan, 2003; Wadiwel, 2009). Though it is more usually linked specifically with studies of gender and sexuality, its central aim is – perhaps surprisingly for some – not to champion what we might describe more broadly as LGBT causes and interests. At its heart, queer theory has a primary interest in favouring diversity by rejecting essentialist framings and fixed identity claims. It is therefore rather suspicious of labels such as gay, lesbian, bisexual, etc., preferring instead to assert the fluid, mutable and diverse nature of gender as a part of identity. Sullivan (2003, p. 43) comments on its aim 'to challenge normative knowledge and identities', while Warner (1993, p. xxvi) sees it as fundamentally linked to 'a thorough resistance to regimes of the normal'. As such, it is concerned with 'pronouncing and enacting counterhegemonic interventions' (Wilton, 2009, p. 507). The reasons for this are described by Barry Adam (2009, p. 306), an early pioneer of queer studies:

We are now in a period when difference is the order of the day, and queer orthodoxy denies the search for, or assertion of, commonality now that the commonality posited by gay/lesbian identities has been exposed as never really having existed....

This position means that it has not always found favour with some LGBT scholars (e.g., Halperin, 2012, p. 63) who counters that 'being gay has been experienced through highly patterned forms of embodied sensibility'. Debating these positions is of course beyond the scope and intentions of this chapter, but it is important to establish some clarity on the key tenets of queer theory. Fraser and Lamble (2014/2015, p. 65) usefully identify what they see as its two core elements – firstly, 'its ethos of questioning and contesting norms' and secondly, its aim to 'disrupt and question normative power relations' in order to highlight nonnormative and alternative possibilities. As such, they present a powerful argument for bringing a queer lens to the business and practice of HE:

In this invocation, queer is not so much a (sexual) identity as it is a practice or a method for questioning the logic of normalcy

(Fraser & Lamble, 2014/2015, p. 65).

Gunn and McAllister (2013) similarly highlight its fundamental concern to denormativise hegemonic architecture, while even Foucault (1996) referred to the slantwise queer position as enabling an alternative way of looking at the world. Drawing on this understanding, then, a queer lens will be used in this chapter, not just in an attempt to question, disrupt and contest what I see as the essentialising hegemonic logics behind the nature and effects of the TEF, but also as a politically generative exercise in opening up space for thinking about possibilities that exceed the established norms.

SCRUTINISING THE TEF

To attempt the above, it is important first of all to examine some of the TEF's key components. Beginning with the rationale for its introduction, its contribution to extending the national conversation about teaching excellence and altering the power dynamic between research and teaching (French & O'Leary, 2017) is clearly of merit. However, these elements arguably take a back seat in the government's own rhetoric which centres more strongly on its aim 'to deliver value to students and taxpayers' (DBIS 2016, p. 6). This consumerist framing is reiterated later on in the same government report:

> *Competition between providers in any market incentivises them to raise their game, offering consumers a greater choice of more innovative and better quality products and services at a lower cost. Higher Education is no exception.*

> *(p. 8)*

Though some elements have been modified since its intro-duction, Gibbs (2017) is among many commentators who remain critical of its unaltered rationale, seeing it as funda-mentally flawed. He argues that the interpretations of evidence about educational quality, employability and value-for-money which are used to justify its operation are irrational and unsuitable for producing reliable judgements. Shattock (2018, p. 21) is similarly critical of the ways in which the metrics and datasets it uses are merged to form judgements of excellence – 'bundled together, this is a statistical mishmash'. Such concerns are in fact much voiced, and Rudd (2017) for one provides an extended analysis of the many and varied critiques of the TEF, echoing many of the chapters in this volume. Much of his critique centres on the TEF's use of data derived from the National Student Survey (NSS) – 'essentially an inappropriate customer survey' (p. 64).

This particular aspect is important because it serves to embed the notion of the student as consumer firmly at the heart of the TEF's rationale. As Frankham (2017, pp. 633–634) rightly points out, 'there has been considerable recent debate on the student as a consumer of HE and how consumer-like behaviour is more evident as a consequence of changes in policy and practices in UK universities'. While the TEF cannot single-handedly be held responsible for this, I would argue that the TEF, with the strong emphasis it places on NSS data based on student satisfaction, plays a large part in cementing such behaviours. Though a concern with satisfaction might seem a benign preoccupation, it is important to consider that the notion is firmly rooted in a business ontology with potentially harmful consequences. Williams (2013, p. 99) provides a detailed analysis of this, arguing that:

> *'Student satisfaction' in effect measures nothing more than how students subjectively feel at a particular point in time; their success on the programme to date (in terms of grades); and the extent to which any demands they have made of lecturers have been met.*

She goes on to discuss how this focus reinforces the idea that the very purpose of HE is to create satisfied consumers, and that this understanding, as it embeds itself in institutional thinking and practices, begins to have maladaptive consequences for pedagogy:

> *The demand to produce satisfied consumers potentially has an impact upon pedagogy, as it may lead some lecturers to avoid making intellectual demands of their students and provide 'entertainment rather than education.'...Lecturers seeking promotion and security are incentivised to make students satisfied through flattery and appeasement.*
>
> *(p. 100)*

As French and O'Leary (2017) identify, one issue here is the fundamental flaw in equating satisfaction with learning. Though there is some connection between the two – and whatever this relationship, it is a very complex, shifting and fluid one – effective and deep learning is often unsettling and challenging, and thus potentially unlikely to be rated by some as 'satisfactory'. But more than this, entrenching this understanding at the heart of HE serves to perpetuate a mono-optical construction of the student as consumer, thereby reducing alternative framings as it normalises and embeds a hegemonic homo economicus identity. It is precisely such essentialising processes that queer theory can help us to expose, contest and disrupt – processes that are tantamount to a relentless (hetero)normativity in the TEF's privileging of consumerist machismo which will now be cross-examined.

THE TEF – CEMENTING CONSUMERIST MACHISMO

As discussed above, the instrumentality enshrined in the TEF logic of prioritising students' evaluations of satisfaction helps to 'construct education as a transaction and students as consumers' (Frankham, 2017, p. 635). In a sense, it could be argued the TEF reflects what Dahler-Larsen (2012, p. 75) describes as contemporary society's obsession with evaluation and its emphasis on user satisfaction 'legitimised by consumerism in society'. In such a climate, 'it is difficult to be against evaluation' (Dahler-Larsen, 2012, p. 3) and universities, as 'public' organisations, 'mostly do what is in accordance with the cultural environment in which they operate' (Dahler-Larsen, 2012, p. 93). The TEF's fetishisation of satisfaction, and the way this influences institutional behaviour, policy and practice, is only one of the four key elements that in my view entrench a narrow, consumerist hegemony. The second feature is the highly visible way in which it operates to reduce the diversity of learning, experience, relationships and purpose behind HE study to a simple gold/silver/bronze quality stamp. This manifests a desire to frame and constrain universities as consumer commodities that can be compared and labelled as easily as cars, holidays or washing powders. As Shattock (2018, p. 22) puts it:

> *The selection of Gold, Silver and Bronze awards can only be described as crude, populist, and pandering to media exploitation.*

From a queer perspective, this parading of colours could be read as a flamboyantly visual attempt to flaunt the TEF's consumerist mission, in a way that is conspicuously out, loud and proud. In addition to fulfilling its function as a consumer branding system, the third element concerns how it simultaneously operates as a mechanism that fetishises and fosters competition as an organising principle for institutions and students. Institutions are incentivised to aim for gold so that they may not only attract a larger share of better qualified students in the competitive market place but also so that they will be in a position to boost income further by raising tuition fees in line with inflation, as only the higher-branded institutions will be allowed to do (Ashwin, 2017). Students too are incentivised to take advantage of this information as a basis for making consumer choices about where best to study and which institutions will allow them to maximise their chances of gaining the 'best degree' and subsequently the 'best employment' options. As such, the logic of the TEF encourages students once again to foreground their economic motives (Bartram, 2016), thereby framing the purpose of HE study firmly within a neoliberal logic of macho, competitive, economic self-interest. A queer lens would once again contest this 'biggest and best' macho-normative framing in order to release rival motives, desires and aspirations from the closet.

The TEF's totalising logic is arguably also promoted by a fourth element – its emphasis on employability within the metrics it utilises, drawing on student employment data post-graduation and, as currently under consideration, incorporating 'actual graduate salaries after five years to be acquired from the tax authorities' (Shattock, 2018, p. 22). Frankham (2017, p. 632) describes how this growing focus on employability 'has also changed the general environment of HE. Universities increasingly have dedicated staff, responsible entirely for employability initiatives, for liaising with employers, for carrying out "skills audits" at the point of graduation and gathering statistics on graduate destinations'. Barkas, Scott, Poppit and Smith (2017, p. 7) argue that even though the whole notion of employability is contested and nebulous, it has become enmeshed in a normalising discourse around HE, as Frankham (2017) demonstrates:

> *...a discourse is created that appears to be normal...; with continued use, an unquestioning acceptance becomes embodied in the language, a process that Bernstein (2000) termed 'normalisation of genericism'.*

Williams (2013, p. 89) echoes similar sentiments, highlighting the special part employability plays in the competition fetish and arguing that 'this relentless promotion of employability is due to a need for institutions to appear attractive to new students by demonstrating the employment success of previous cohorts'. It is not my intention here to argue there is no link between degree study and employment, or that securing a job post-graduation is an unimportant consideration – but as we see in Barkas et al.'s argument – and indeed, through a queer lens – this relentless discourse contributes to the normalisation of a narrow set of expectations and understandings of the university and its purposes and as such becomes part of an armoury that privileges a normative fixation with macho metrics, while 'othering' and subordinating alternative ways of thinking, acting and desiring in the contemporary academy.

'TEFFECTS' OF THE MACHO MONOLITH

The above section makes the case for the role the TEF plays in cementing the monolithic neoliberal framework within which UK HE is firmly constructed, based on what I see as four key elements. A queer analysis would suggest that together these features combine to create and normalise an essentialist student-consumer identity. Such an assertion naturally invites discussion of why this could be considered problematic – the focus of the next section.

To begin with, its fetishisation of satisfaction may have a number of consequences that do little to support the 'traditional' aims of HE, let alone some of the aspects the TEF was intended to achieve. Williams (2013) above suggests how the prioritisation of satisfaction may ultimately reduce the quality and challenge of education, for example, by encouraging some lecturers to diminish the overall student experience. She illustrates how this reductive risk operates:

> *The notion of being responsive to student choice reinforces the suggestion that lecturers exist to provide a satisfactory service to students rather than an experience that is intellectually challenging, complex and potentially transformative*

(p. 99).

Frankham (2017, p. 635) supports this view, explaining that 'course material that is challenging, and assignments which present students with a challenge are clear foci for student expressions of dissatisfaction and concern [...] this may be diminishing the intellectual challenge of a university degree and the benefits that such a challenge may bring'. As I have argued elsewhere (see Bartram, 2016), such nurturing of satisfaction can further encourage a degree of passivity among students, as they become conditioned to see HE as a form of service provision and themselves as entitled consumers. Such passivity is strongly at odds with the need for active and independent engagement that constitutes effective learning at university level. That said, the same consumer mindset has been implicated in a rather more active orientation when it comes to students investing increasing energies in standing up for their entitlements to satisfactory service, particularly when perceived in relation to such 'products' as grades and classifications – Garner (2009) has noted, for example, how dissatisfaction with assessment and degree outcomes has seen a strong increase in student complaints at UK universities. More broadly, Frankham also discusses how the need noted by staff in her research to cultivate student contentment has engendered a stronger degree of student dependence on staff – 'students are becoming less independent, perhaps less capable of initiative, perhaps less capable of thinking for themselves, over time' (p. 636). A participant in Bartram's (2018, p. 276) study echoes the very same sentiment:

> ... *the increase in tuition fees has led not only to consumer practices amongst students but an over eager approach from the university to recruit and retain students, regardless of conduct or working quality. There has been a notable increase in student support services coupled with altered grading criteria whereby students are by large spoon fed information. The culture has increased students' dependence rather than independence.*

If we go along with this interpretation, then, it could be argued that the TEF – ironically – is doing little to support universities in their attempts to develop graduate orientations that enhance student employability. In the same study, Bartram (2018, p. 276) also notes how increased institutional courting of student satisfaction via such mechanisms as the NSS and TEF appeared to be 'central elements in encouraging emotional bargaining', whereby some students exhibit an increasing tendency to make strategic use of their emotions in exchange for a range of academic concessions and improved outcomes.

Alongside such arguably reductive effects on students, Williams (2013) also points out what she sees as a negative influence of the employability agenda that the TEF promotes on university courses themselves. She argues forcefully that the fixation with employment has led to teaching staff being encouraged to present the vocational importance of what they teach to students above academic merits and cites examples of a philosophy degree at Exeter University incorporating a 'Humanities in the Workplace' module (2013, p. 89), seeing such a development in strongly critical terms:

> *If studying an academic subject cannot be justified because it makes an essential contribution to our collective understanding of what it means to be human and the nature of the society we live in, it must instead justify its existence in the more mundane sphere of employability.*

It is again beyond the scope of this chapter to debate the relative merits of such developments, though the above example arguably illustrates the narrowing impact of the neoliberal university vision. Heaney and Mackenzie (2017), who see the TEF very much as a mechanism of control, expose two further reductive effects. Not only is it likely to reduce the breadth of the pedagogical diet students experience – 'under perpetual pedagogical control, peda-gogical exploration becomes totally subordinated to the production of satisfied and employable customers' (p. 13) – but also it may ultimately end up reducing the range of university degree courses available to students, thereby ironically reducing consumer choice, as universities become inclined to remove courses perceived to be associated with lower levels of satisfaction or post-graduation employment. And even more worryingly perhaps, Furedi (2017) argues the most significant effect of such mechanisms as the NSS and TEF is the way in which they operate to diminish capacity. He suggests that the culture of courting satisfaction which they engender and the various forms of 'institutional flattery' (p. 140) which naturally follow ultimately infantilise stu-dents and reduce their capacity for dealing with challenge and ambiguity.

From these combined 'TEFfects', the picture of students that emerges is – arguably – an unflattering one: diminished and passive, inclined to massage by metrics, seduced by dataset desires and employment promise and addicted to easy and narrow satisfactions. Viewed through a queer lens, these effects might be seen as the inevitable outcomes of a crushing and stifling (hetero)normative ontology that fixates on and fetishises consumerist logics at the expense of other ways of being, thinking and wanting.

MOVING FORWARD WITH A QUEER EYE

So far, then, I have argued that the TEF operates to normalise a macho consumerist identity, consistent with the neoliberal philosophy of 'closing off alternative approaches' (Saunders, 2015, p. 403). It does this by locating HE firmly within a masculinist business ontology, whereby institutions, lecturers and students are systematically conditioned into compliance with a consumerist vision of universities that redefines how we come to see their purpose, the ways in which we judge their worth, and indeed how we behave and engage. Rudd (2017, p. 73) explains how once such a vision has become embedded:

> *A powerful new 'doxa' (Bourdieu, 1984) may arise that will result in compliance to the new wider discourse and newly constructed 'realities', both through conscious resignation, and more efficiently, through unconscious compliance. This may be precisely the moment we are at with regard to the Higher Education and Research Act, and particularly the TEF.*

A queer analysis would concur that the TEF has helped to perpetuate and privilege this consumer doxa and that cross-examining its essentialising assumptions and reductive effects in order to denormativise its hegemonic control is part of queer theory's raison d'être. As Warner (1993, p. xxvi) suggested above, queer theory aims above all to resist 'regimes of the normal', and this chapter has hopefully demonstrated that the TEF has very quickly become part of 'the HE normal', in the process closing down, eclipsing and othering what might be described as non-normative student constructions and ways of being and wanting. Queer theory is therefore of service in helping to formulate a counterstance against the TEF's narrowly singular, neoliberal hegemony – but can it go beyond this position? In other words, how can we use it not simply to expose its macho consumerist logic, but, as Wilton (2009) suggests, to find constructive ways of undermining its philosophy and effects?

To this end, queer theory can help us to reflect on alternative orientations and possibilities, given its concern with diversity and contesting the very notion of normalcy – and with recognising, liberating, including and nurturing alternative desires, motives and ways of being. In this sense, queer theory can usefully remind tutors of their importance in allowing, exploring and encouraging other student motives and identities. Though this is admittedly no simple task, staff should grasp opportunities that allow them to address what Hull (2002, p. 19) sees as the key challenge teachers face:

> *The teaching problem is not one of developing students' reasoning powers [...] Rather, the teacher's problem is to help awaken desire at its deepest level. The solution involves developing students' capacity for openness and receptivity to their own and to one another's hearts, minds and passions.*

This challenge is unlikely to be supported by a TEF-driven system that fetishises user satisfaction and competition.

Fraser and Lamble (2014/2015, p. 64) emphasise how queer theory can be enlisted not just to question but also as 'a method of dreaming, naming and being otherwise in the world'. Quoting Munoz (2009, p. 1), they show us how a queer view can help educators contemplate approaches to teaching and learning that genuinely challenge and open:

> Queerness is a structuring and educated mode of desiring that allows us to see and feel beyond the quagmire of the present.... We must dream and enact new and better pleasures, other ways of being in the world, and ultimately new worlds. Queerness is a longing that propels us onward, beyond romances of the negative and toiling in the present. Queerness is that thing that lets us feel that this world is not enough, that indeed something is missing....
> Queerness is essentially about the rejection of a here and now and an insistence on potentiality or concrete possibility for another world.

It is my contention that the TEF is a part of this 'quagmire of the present', suffocating better pleasures, discriminating against alternative desires and closeting potentiality. Clearly, queer theory's contribution to disrupting the logics of the TEF will not lie in establishing a prescriptive set of simple measures or strategies, but in adopting a stance that encourages educators to reflect on how they engage in practices with students that enable, broaden and transform, rather than reproduce and comply with dominant educational scripts and political orthodoxy. As Fraser and Lamble (2014/2015, p. 68) quite rightly point out, adopting such a stance 'does not require us to identify as queer or to be experts in queer theory. It simply asks that we be open to practices that foster space for different types of desires to flourish'. They do, however, suggest that a practice they describe as 'queering conversation' can be a useful strategy for enacting this vision. For them, queer conversation is based on three key attributes (2015, p. 68–69):

- a continual questioning and disruption of the conventional binary between teacher and student;

- the disruption of norms around the boundaries of what can and cannot be said in the classroom;

- the capacity to make space for new potentialities and possibilities.

Queering the TEF would therefore involve teachers in a careful and constant mission (and mindset) that seeks to allow students to bring nonutilitarian desires out of the closet and experiment with different ways of enjoying university; to queer the service provider/user binary; to remind students of the life-long humanistic 'gains' that being at university can offer – the friendships; the social benefits and pleasures; the personal enrichment; the transformative power of shifting horizons; the joys and challenges of new ways of thinking and sharing; the development of rich interior resources; in short, the need to nurture a dynamic diversity of satisfactions, pleasures and motives. In some senses, these ideas chime with Wood's (2017) discussion of 'emergent pedagogies' and fostering approaches that could be adopted to subvert the TEF. The challenges involved here in the context of the neoliberalized university landscape are not insignificant – as discussed, HE policy in general and the TEF in particular position students primarily as consumers, conditioned to internalise an individualised, economically focused, competitive macho subjectivity. Resisting the weight of these collective neoliberal influences is no mean feat, and some may suggest that the queer challenge mounted in this chapter will do little to disrupt the stranglehold which the TEF maintains. In this respect, Fraser and Lamble (2014/2015, p. 74) sound a note of optimism:

> *For us these strategies are about making small changes in order to open spaces for bigger ones; they are about doing transformative politics at the micro-relational level in order to question and rethink power at the structural or systemic level. [...] Despite their ephemeral quality, they can shift a course, alter a student's engagement, and bring about the generative spark that ignites the potentialities students bring to the classroom.*

Queering the TEF by adopting approaches that repeatedly engage students in expansive ways of thinking and desiring, then, could not only serve to enhance the mission of the university as a 'public' good that genuinely enriches us all but also it may help to expose and undermine the worst effects of the TEF and – to finish with a filmic flourish, if I may – to begin to move UK HE from the stark machismo of Quentin Tarantino to the gentler sensibilities of Quentin Crisp.

REFERENCES

Adam, B. (2009). How might we create a collectivity that we would want to belong to? In Halperin, D. & Traub, V. (Eds.), *Gay shame*. Chicago, IL: University of Chicago Press, 301–311.

Ashwin, P. (2017). What is the Teaching Excellence Framework in the United Kingdom, and will it work?. *International Higher Education*, *88*(Winter), 10–11.

Barkas, L., Scott, J., Poppitt, N., & Smith, P. (2017). Tinker, tailor, policy-maker: Can the UK government's teaching excellence framework deliver its objectives?. *Journal of Further and Higher Education.* doi:10.1080/0309877X.2017.1408789.

Bartram, B. (2016). Economic motives to attend university: A cross-country study. *Research in Post-Compulsory Education, 21*(4), 394–408.

Bartram, B. (2018). University students and emotional bargaining: A comparative study of staff perspectives in Northern Europe. *Research in Post-Compulsory Education, 23*(2), 266–283.

Bernstein, B. (2000). *Pedagogy, symbolic control and identity.* London: Taylor and Francis.

Bourdieu, P. (1984). *Distinction: A social critique of the judgement of taste.* London: Routledge.

Dahler-Larsen, P. (2012). *The evaluation society.* Stanford, CA: Stanford University Press.

Department for Business Innovation and Skills (2016). *Success as a knowledge economy: Teaching excellence, social mobility and student choice.* London: DBIS.

Foucault, M. (1996). Friendship as a way of life. In *Foucault live: Interviews, 1966–84* (pp. 204–207). Boston, MA: The MIT Press.

Frankham, J. (2017). Employability and higher education: The follies of the 'productivity challenge' in the teaching excellence framework. *Journal of Education Policy, 32*(5), 628–641.

Fraser, J., & Lamble, S. (2014/2015). Queer desires and critical pedagogies in higher education: Reflections on the transformative potential of non-normative learning desires in the classroom. *Journal of Feminist Scholarship, 7/8,* 61–77.

French, A., & O'Leary, M. (2017). *Teaching excellence in higher education: Challenges, changes and the teaching excellence framework*. Bingley: Emerald Publishing Limited.

Furedi, F. (2017). *What's happened to the university? A sociological exploration of its infantilisation*. Abingdon: Routledge.

Garner, R. (2009). Why are students complaining so much, and do they have a case? *The Independent*, 20 May.

Gibbs, G. (2017). Evidence does not support the rationale of the TEF. *Compass: Journal of Learning and Teaching*, *10*(2), 1–10.

Gunn, V., & McAllister, C. (2013). Methods on the margins? Queer theory as method in higher education research. In (Ed.), *Theory and method in higher education research: International perspectives on higher education research* (Vol. 9, pp. 155–174). Bingley: Emerald Publishing Limited.

Halperin, D. (2012). *How to be gay*. Cambridge, MA: Belknap Press of Harvard University Press.

Heaney, C., & Mackenzie, H. (2017). The teaching excellence framework: Perpetual pedagogical control in postwelfare capitalism. *Compass: Journal of Learning and Teaching*, *10*(2), 1–17.

Hull, K. (2002). Eros and education: The role of desire in teaching and learning. *NEA Higher Education Journal*, *18*, 19–31.

Munoz, J. (2009). *Cruising utopia: The then and there of queer futurity*. New York, NY: New York University Press.

OfS. (2018). What is the TEF? Retrieved from https://www.officeforstudents.org.uk/advice-and-guidance/teaching/what-is-the-tef/

Rudd, T. (2017). TEF: Re-examining its logic and considering possible systemic and institutional outcomes. *Journal of Critical Education Policy Studies*, 2(15), 59–90.

Saunders, D. (2015). Resisting excellence: Challenging neoliberal ideology in postsecondary education. *Journal for Critical Education Policy Studies*, 12(2), 391–411.

Shattock, M. (2018). Better informing the market? The teaching excellence framework (TEF) in British higher education. *International Higher Education*, 92(Winter), 21–22.

Sullivan, N. (2003). *A critical introduction to queer theory*. Edinburgh: Edinburgh University Press.

Wadiwel, D. (2009). Sex and the lubricative ethic. In N. Giffney & M. O'Rourke (Eds.), *The Ashgate research companion to queer theory* (pp. 491–506). Farnham: Ashgate Publishing.

Warner, M. (1993). Introduction. In M. Warner (Ed.), *Fear of a queer planet: Queer politics and social theory*. Minneapolis, MN: University of Minnesota Press.

Williams, J. (2013). *Consuming higher education: Why learning can't be bought*. London: Bloomsbury.

Wilton, T. (2009). All Foucault and no knickers: Assessing claims for a queer-political erotics. In N. Giffney & M. O'Rourke (Eds.), *The Ashgate research companion to queer theory* (pp. 507–522). Farnham: Ashgate Publishing.

Wood, P. (2017). From teaching excellence to emergent pedagogies: A complex process alternative to understanding the role of teaching in higher education. In A. French & M. O'Leary (Eds.), *Teaching excellence in higher education: Challenges, changes and the teaching excellence framework*. Bingley: Emerald Publishing Limited.

7

DIVERSITY DEFICITS: RESISTING THE TEF

Andrew Brogan

ABSTRACT

This chapter draws on Michel de Certeau's work on strategies and tactics to critique the Teaching Excellence Framework (TEF) and, importantly, suggests a form of creative resistance to it. The TEF operates as a strategy of English higher education to reduce teaching and learning to quantifiable proxy measures which are then used to hold academics' performance to account. The selection and use of these proxy measures introduces a specific relationship between academics and students rooted in the underlying neoliberal principles of exchange and private gain, reducing HE teaching and learning to a provider–consumer relationship. In defiance of this academics need to utilise increasingly creative tactics to enable them to conform to the requirements of the TEF while simultaneously resisting and subverting this provider–consumer relationship. De Certeau's work on la perruque, *or wiggery, as alternative tactics disguised as work for an employer offers us a*

way to counter the pervasive presence of TEF. La perruque *encourages us to make use of the structures and
places provided to us by higher education institutions to
make something alien to them, for example, reorganis-
ing classroom spaces in such a way that does not prioritise the presence of the lecturer or designing sessions
and modules starting from existing student knowledge
rather than assuming a deficit to be addressed. Each of
these tactics of resistance is fleeting and temporary, but
each provides academics with a creative possibility to
navigate the tensions of neoliberal provider–consumer
relationships on the one hand and collaborative
knowledge production on the other.*

Keywords: TEF; resistance; *La perruque*; wiggery;
tactics; strategies

> *If it is true that the grid of 'discipline' is everywhere
> becoming clearer and more extensive, it is all the
> more urgent to discover how an entire society resists
> being reduced to it, what popular procedures (also
> 'miniscule' and quotidian) manipulate the
> mechanisms of discipline and conform to them only
> in order to evade them [...].*

De Certeau, 1988, p. xiv

In this short passage, the French social theorist Michel
de Certeau is criticising the systems of power which seek to
control society through disciplinary measures and look for
ways in which people resist these systems of power. While
written in the late 1980s, this post-structuralist framing of

the issue of power and resistance is just as relevant today as individuals face a myriad of increasingly complex ensembles of power and attempts to control society through a wide variety of means (Amoore, 2013). These attempts range from the overt observation and policing of behaviour through CCTV and security systems, to covert digital data collection and algorithms used to collate information about movements, shopping habits and leisure time (Amoore, 2013). De Certeau's use of the term 'discipline' refers to Michel Foucault's (1977) exploration of the diffuse nature of power and the possibilities to resist it. Both philosophers concerned themselves with an interrogation of the world that they saw as an increasingly complex set of practices aiming to control behaviour and the theorisation and implementation of individual and collective responses to those practices. De Certeau's quote serves as a touchstone for this chapter and a rallying cry for political thought and action.

In this chapter I analyse the Teaching Excellence Framework (TEF) as a regulatory practice required by English higher education institutions and the actions of academics in enacting possible forms of resistance to the TEF by drawing on de Certeau's twin notions of strategies and tactics. My analysis starts with the argument that UK higher education institutions operate as part of a larger neoliberal framework which in the past two decades has seen substantial changes, including a shift to a younger student body and variations in financing through higher tuition fees and a drop in funding grants (Universities UK, 2015). The UK government paper *Success as a Knowledge Economy* in 2016 introduced yet more changes including the increased marketisation of higher education, the role of HEIs as service providers and a student–teacher relationship based on provider–consumer economic logic

(Brogan, 2017; Department for Business, Innovation & Skills, 2016). A central aspect of these changes is the TEF which represents an explicit attempt to control the behaviour of teaching active academics through the lens of a neoliberal economic logic. This logic seeks to reduce judgements of excellent teaching to a set of proxy measures like student satisfaction, student outcomes and graduate employment (French & O'Leary, 2017).

Approaching the TEF through de Certeau's work, the TEF is a strategy through which UK universities orient and define themselves in relation to institutions exterior to them, as well as defining and orienting the practices of academics within the institutions themselves.[1] Operating both externally and internally, the TEF encourages higher education institutions to have a myopic focus on processes of measurement and accounting, despite the well-documented challenges with this approach. My concern and contention in this chapter echoes the words of de Certeau above: namely that the imposition of the TEF reduces the notion of excellent teaching to a set of proxy measures, which must and can be resisted. If we, as academics, allow teaching and learning in higher education to become reduced to student satisfaction, contact hours or graduate employment, we do ourselves and students a disservice. Teaching and learning in higher education is about the collaborative construction of knowledge and the growth and expansion of society and its members: this is not something that can be captured through accounting, bureaucracy and ranking. And yet, we academics work in these institutions, are held accountable to these proxy measures and are complicit – however reluctantly – in their continuation. This chapter is concerned with exploring how we are able to

---

1 Such as government, businesses, other universities and educational institutions.

navigate this tension between the demands of the TEF and the economic logic underpinning it and the desire to engage in collaborative knowledge construction. The questions at the heart of this chapter ape de Certeau's language and are concerned with how we as academics can manipulate the TEF and conform to it only to evade it. How can we as academics resist the attempts to control our actions while still being enmeshed in those systems of control?

To this end the chapter proceeds in three movements. The first is an exploration of de Certeau's concept of 'strategies' which serves as the theoretical foundations for an understanding of and possible resistance to the TEF. The second movement is concerned with the use of tactics in resisting the TEF in the classroom: a development of de Certeau's *la perruque* (1988, p. 25) or 'wiggery' (Heilbronn, 2013, p. 36), which demonstrate practical ways of resistance. In the final movement we explore the necessary creativity involved in 'wiggery' and the use of this creativity in classroom tactics, which enables us to play in the tensions of our positions in higher education rather than being paralysed by them. The chapter concludes with hints of possibilities of resistance drawn from personal experience.

STRATEGIES AND PLACES

To understand the TEF as a strategy of higher education institutions, one first needs to explore the role of strategies in de Certeau's work. De Certeau writes:

> *I call a strategy the calculation (or manipulation) of power relationships that becomes possible as soon as a subject with will and power (a business, an army, a*

> *city, a scientific institution) can be isolated. It*
> *postulates a place that can be determined as its own*
> *and serve as the base from which relations with an*
> *exteriority composed of targets or threats (customers*
> *or competitors, enemies, the country surrounding the*
> *city, objectives, objects of research, etc.) can be*
> *managed.*

(de Certeau, 1988, p. 35–36).

For de Certeau, strategies are attempts to control the people's actions by creating places of conformity. Institutions like universities use strategies to establish areas of control by demarcating exterior actors with which they interact and parcelling out interior spaces through a 'panoptic practice' (de Certeau, 1988, p. 36) in which each interior actor is held in a specific position and relation to other interior actors. These exterior actors include other universities, businesses, local community groups, media groups and local, regional and national political structures. The interior actors include faculties, schools and departments within universities, as well as taught degree programmes, individual modules and individual academics. Looking both outward and inward, the university locates these different actors in positions which can be observed, measured and accounted for in the attempt to bring a stability and control to the university (de Certeau, 1988, p. 36). This stability is introduced through a rigid application of specific places where one actor and their behaviours cannot overlap with another (de Certeau, 1988, p. 117), meaning that two actors cannot occupy the same place at the same time. The idea of place has an important role in de Certeau's strategies as it is through the control and manipulation of actors externally and internally that institutions like universities are able to deploy strategies with such effect.

We can use these notions of strategies and places to analyse the relationship between higher education institutions and TEF. In this analysis, higher education institutions are the 'subject with will and power' (de Certeau, 1988, p. 35), which establishes a place from which they operate both physically and in the abstract. UK higher education institutions draw borderlines to separate themselves from others. The markers of this border are the elements of the university tasked specifically with managing relations with exterior actors, for example, marketing departments, media-trained academics, research funding applications and, of course, the TEF.

In many cases a university's internal place has a physical form of a campus or a set of buildings with controlled access limited to those who are part of that institution, as students, lecturers or support services. Once in these physical locations, the specific places of these interior actors within the institution are carefully managed in relation to one another. There are not only places in which the individual groups, be they students, academics or others, are separated, but also places in which they are meant to interact and expected forms of behaviour guiding that interaction: lecture theatres, seminar rooms, etc. One way of controlling the behaviour of different actors within the physical institution of the university is to define the places each actor can occupy and to make it clear that different places require different behaviours. In the case of the classroom, the university establishes a location which positions the lecturer at the front of the room by the lectern or the whiteboard and sets the students on tables and chairs about the room, most often in rows or squares. This establishment of location in the classroom reinforces an understanding of teaching and learning which assigns the lecturer as the arbiter of knowledge and the students as recipients.

Strategies are those procedures that make an institution knowable to the exterior while simultaneously aiding the institution in maintaining the internal order of place. The TEF is the primary strategy of the UK higher education institution: externally the TEF operates in unison and overlapping with other strategies like the Research Excellence Framework (REF), the National Student Survey (NSS) and different league tables to present a particular and managed image of the university beyond its boundaries. It does this through the provision of easily recognisable colour-coded awards of bronze, silver or gold. Potential students, employers, other institutions and others external to the university are told that the awarding of a particular TEF status ostensibly conveys all they need to know about the quality of the teaching and learning which occurs in this particular university. Through the TEF, the university makes itself known to others beyond its boundaries and locates itself within a larger societal framework which assigns the university value through the lens of potential economic gain for the individual student. The TEF functions as a watermark of quality, a public review of a product in much the same way as we may turn to star ratings on Amazon or TripAdvisor to help us make decisions about where to spend our money in the hope for the best return possible – whether that is a superior consumer product or a particular holiday 'experience'.

The TEF also operates as the primary internal strategy for higher education institutions, playing a guiding role in the internal organisation of relationships and actions within the university, ensuring each actor is held in their proper place in relation to another and is acting in the expected ways. This internal organising role of the TEF is particularly apparent in the relationship and behaviours it prioritises between the institution and lecturers. To explore this relationship and actions we need to recap what exactly the TEF measures when measuring teaching quality, as it is this series of metrics that establishes the basis of the relationship between institution and lecturer and the expected actions for lecturers. The TEF uses proxy measures for teaching excellence which include student satisfaction, student outcomes and employment rates following graduation (Department for Business, Innovation & Skills 2016, p. 46). Each of these proxy measures – which are not without their issues as individual metrics, let alone as a collection – establishes expected actions of lecturers in their day-to-day lives in the institution (French & O'Leary 2017). Through the TEF institutional concerns with student satisfaction, student outcomes and graduate employment take precedence over the traditional university focus on the pursuit and creation of knowledge and the importance of student learning. Increasingly, the above metrics are institutionalised as internal performance metrics for individual lecturers, building on the notion of academic performativity (Ball, 2012). The metrics become the procedure by which higher education institutions organise and manage the actions of academics and determine the relationship between the institution and the academic. The metrics of the TEF are *the* strategy through which a higher education institution manages lecturers as part of the pursuit of a high TEF status which then enables the institution to promote and maintain itself as a place, as a subject with will and power.

Following de Certeau's work we have demonstrated how higher education institutions can be approached as subjects with will and power maintaining a place in distinction to external others and internally organising a place for constituent elements within it. Alongside this it has been shown how the TEF operates as *the* strategy simultaneously addressing the external and internal actors of the university, whether that is through using the TEF as the strategy by which it makes itself known and accountable to external others or by using the TEF and its metrics as the organising principle guiding the management of lecturers in the pursuit of the externally recognisable statuses of bronze, silver or gold. This understanding of higher education institutions and the TEF brings us back to the question posed earlier in the chapter: how can we as academics manipulate the mechanisms of the TEF and conform to them in order to evade them?

TACTICS AND SPACES

At the heart of de Certeau's concept of strategy is the attempt to control people through the creation of places of conformity: de Certeau writes of this attempt using the language of production and consumption. Production and consumption are not confined to economics in de Certeau's work, but carry a much broader meaning, including the production and consumption of culture and the production and consumption of societal practices (de Certeau, 1988). By way of an illustration of de Certeau's understanding of the relation between production and consumption, we can consider television programming: TV shows are largely made to entertain or inform, or with the increasing prevalence of online streaming services, captivate and totalise an audience's attention and time. Yet, there is no guarantee that the intended aim is how these TV shows are consumed in practice. The audience may indeed watch episode after episode of a newly released box set, but they can do this without giving it their full attention by combining watching the television show with other actions, be that, eating, drinking, completing household chores or talking with friends and family. The nature of the activities undertaken whilst watching TV is not important, the point is that other actions can be and are performed, and there is no way for the television producer to enforce a viewer's full attention. This signifies an important gap between production and consumption.

The television example may appear fairly benign, but it sets the ground for approaching the TEF as something which is produced with one aim in mind, but can be consumed differently. The TEF as a strategy of higher education institutions is part of a move to further integrate UK universities into neoliberal market logic and to determine the actions of academics through a focus on student satisfaction, student outcomes and graduate employment, among others. In the pursuit of a Gold TEF status, English higher education institutions have to adopt and maximise their performance in these metrics as internal forms of organisation and in order to account for lecturer performance, with the place, relationships and actions of the lecturer becoming oriented by the TEF. However, as with the television example above, English higher education institutions cannot completely close the gap between the production of the TEF metrics and the assigned locations and behaviours of academics. On the contrary, the university's myopic focus on TEF as *the* strategy used to determine and maintain itself as a place enables a gap between the production of the TEF and the aim with which it was designed and its consumption and the way it is used by academics in the classroom. As higher education institutions seek to impose ever-stricter modes of organisation on academics, they inadvertently create blind spots: those areas of academic practice which fall outside the concentrated focus of the TEF metrics. In order for us to conform to the TEF and simultaneously exploit and play in the gap, we need to develop tactics which can create subversive spaces in the classroom by developing academic practice which is entirely alien to the wider strategy of the TEF. Any possible resistance to the TEF therefore lies in this gap between production and consumption, a gap explored and exploited through various tactics.

In contrast to a strategy as a form of control, a tactic is 'a calculated action determined by the absence of a proper locus. No delimitation of an exteriority provides it with the conditions necessary for autonomy. The space of a tactic is the space of the other' (de Certeau, 1988, p. 36–37). Where strategy aims for conformity and maintains a certain bounded space as its locus, tactics lack such boundaries and fixed focal point. Lacking this fixed focal point tactics do not require the exterior actors of strategies – the universities, businesses, local community groups and alike from above – in order to operate. Instead, with the lack of a definite focal point, tactics can operate anywhere. De Certeau explains that tactics always play on and with the 'terrain imposed on it' (de Certeau, 1988, p. 37) and as such operate in continuously isolated instances. This transient nature of tactics means that they can never consolidate a position and can never plan particular practices, but instead must seize moments as they arise and be forever on the lookout for any possible gaps between production and expected consumption (de Certeau, 1988, p. 37). So, if strategy seeks to create protected places in which all possibilities are controlled and accounted for in favour of the predominant forms of social relationships and actions, tactics seek to create spaces that subvert these expected relationships and actions. Buchanan summarises tactics as 'being constantly in the swim of things and are as much in danger of being swept away or submerged by the flow of events as they are capable of bursting through the dykes' (2000, p. 89).

In the fleeting and momentary development of tactics, we, HE lecturers in this instance, can create spaces: a physically and temporally limited area which is embedded within and yet paradoxically separate from the university as an established place. De Certeau explains that spaces occur because of certain practices that 'orient it, situate it [and] temporalize it' (Buchanan, 2000, p. 117), lending space a greater fluidity than place. The tactics that orient, situate and temporalise mean that spaces are constantly in formation and dissolution creating a state of instability and unpredictability in contrast to controlled places. This also means that space is a 'practiced place' (Buchanan, 2000, p. 117), a location which is brought into being by the very actions that both require and constitute it.

The symbiotic concepts of tactics and spaces operate within strategies and places but are separate from them, like a bubble in liquid. It is these notions of tactics and spaces which offer us possibilities to resist the TEF as the strategy of higher education institutions. While tactics and spaces offer us a starting point, we need to explore another part of de Certeau's work to help us better understand what such tactics may look like. In his exploration of how to resist the practices of everyday life, de Certeau introduces us to the tactic of *la perruque* or 'the wig'. *La perruque* is a French term for 'the worker's own work disguised as work for his employer' (de Certeau, 1988, p. 25) and de Certeau illustrates this concept with two examples: the furniture maker and the secretary. A furniture maker uses the lathe at work, scraps of wood and parts of her work time to build a sideboard for her home. This is a creative act on the part of the furniture maker, which is not driven by economic considerations of selling the sideboard and making a profit, but by a desire to make the item for her own use and pleasure. A secretary uses a pen, paper and work time to write a love letter. Again, the love letter is written for the secretary and carries no financial motive. Crucially, *la perruque* is different from both, stealing, as nothing of material value is taken, and absenteeism, as the worker is still present at her job. In both cases, people make use of the dominant frameworks in which they work to produce something entirely unaccountable for by those frameworks and neither action is motivated by an economic concern and directed towards profit (Buchanan, 2000, p. 25). De Certeau points out that this subversive behaviour is not always tolerated and that turning a blind eye to its occurrence has become less common as the attempts to control the gap between production and consumption have increased. But, there are still 'sleights of hand' (Buchanan, 2000, p. 28) available to us as we divert time which is owed to institutions in order to produce other objects and engage in actions that subvert by bypassing the predetermined aim of the dominant political and social frameworks of society (Buchanan, 2000, p. 28). De Certeau argues that *la perruque* is one among many tactics that 'introduce *artistic* tricks and competitions of *accomplices* into a system. [...] Sly as a fox and twice as quick: there are countless ways of "making do"' (de Certeau, 1988, p. 29, original emphasis). It is this sense of creativity that we need to embrace in our attempts to simultaneously conform to and resist the TEF: we need to both discover and create sleights of hand.

While de Certeau addressed the role of *la perruque* as a subversive tactic which could be utilised in and through any manner of strategies, his work does not fully capture the power present in such an approach. *La perruque* reveals itself as a uniquely flexible and nuanced tactic of resistance which avoids a reduction to dichotomies of position/opposition by embracing the tensions we face in everyday life. Ruth Heilbronn has taken de Certeau's ideas and used them to explore the tensions which arise between many school teachers' vocational aims of student learning and growth and the institutional aims of target-driven ends and assessment (Heilbronn, 2013, pp. 31–32). Heilbronn argues that teachers rarely seem to question the broader institutional strategies they are working in, adding that this is entirely reasonable because 'to ask fundamental questions of one's daily work could lead to a loss of faith in that work, in the sense of removing the ladder one is standing on' (Heilbronn, 2013, p. 35). A key responsibility for teacher educators is to assist teachers in being able to question their positions and situations without jeopardising their ability to act. The ethical imperative for teacher educators is to help teachers to cope with living with contradictions (Heilbronn, 2013, p. 36–37). The primary means for dealing with these tensions come through teachers developing a 'strategic competence' (Heilbronn, 2013, p. 35) about the institution they work in and then the ability to engage in *la perruque*, translated by Heilbronn as 'wiggery' (Heilbronn, 2013, p. 36). Highlighting, as de Certeau does, that wiggery is not unethical behaviour, Heilbronn suggests that it is instead playful, creative and witty and that it is this playfulness that is vital for teachers' ability to navigate the tensions in their daily lives and resist the overwhelming pressures of the institution: 'Playfulness enables and announces that alternative viewpoints exist, even if these alternative viewpoints are not fully rationalised' (Heilbronn, 2013, p. 36). *La perruque* enables teachers to hold, and at times pursue, different aims to the institution withosut confronting the authority of the institution head-on (Heilbronn, 2013, p. 36). *La perruque* for teachers can be a subversive and tension-releasing act without necessarily drawing the attention of the institution and negatively impacting on their own position.

We can follow in Heilbronn's footsteps in addressing the tensions faced by academics in higher education institutions. Higher education institutions operate within a larger neoliberal social framework based on economic exchange and the pursuit of individual gain, a key part of signalling their position in and adherence to this social framework is through the TEF as a strategy. As above, the TEF acts as an external face and an internal means of organisation, becoming the primary means by which the actions of academics are monitored, assessed and managed. But what if we as academics do not want our teaching and actions reduced to the TEF metrics? Rather than being paralysed by the TEF as a strategy and the larger neoliberal framework in which English higher education institutions operate, let us embrace creative, witty and playful wiggery to explore those alternative viewpoints to higher education by changing our classroom practice in ways that are not, and cannot be, accounted for by the TEF.

CREATIVE SUBVERSION

The aim of this final section of the chapter is to offer suggestions and possibilities for exploiting the blind spots of the institutional focus on the TEF. The above exploration of strategies and tactics provides a theoretical constellation through which we can approach English higher education institutions, the TEF, and the possibilities for subversion through our actions as academics. Our next step is to address what these practices of wiggery may look like in our everyday academic lives. To help us explore this creative resistance, I consider the classroom layout and our position within it, our interactions with students and collaborative module design, each offering a way to meet the requirements of the TEF while simultaneously, and indirectly, resisting it.

The classroom in higher education institutions is the place in which most student–lecturer interactions take place and the focal point of many of the TEF metrics. Many higher education institutions share a similar set of physical features: tables, chairs, whiteboard, lectern, projector board. The exact position of tables and chairs for the students may vary but the overall orientation of the room is fairly common with the attention focussed on the whiteboard, lectern and projector board. In other words, those pieces of furniture are primarily the domain of the lecturer. This orientation is intended to focus students' attention on the lecturer, explicitly reinforcing the notion that the lecturer is the provider and arbiter of knowledge in the classroom. Even when conversation and debate is encouraged in such a space, contributions are directed to the lecturer who then becomes a living echo, repeating the point back to the students in order to garner the next response. In combination with the layout of the classroom, the corporeal presence of the lecturer herself reinforces the idea that teaching and learning emanate from the lecturer. bell hooks (1994) and Ron Scapp encourage us to address our corporal presence in the classroom. Exploring their two different physical presences in the classroom, hooks as a black woman and Scapp as a white man, they consider what it means for lecturers to be aware of their physical presence – their bodies being imbued with history and particular positions in social structures – in the classroom. In the case of my own physical presence in the classroom, I cannot ignore the social and educational authority that is assumed to come with my position as a tall, white male academic and the impact my physical presence might have on the mainly female and ethnically diverse groups I work with. hooks and Scapp remind us that there is no binary mind/ body split at work in academia and that it is not possible to claim a detached and disembodied knowledge to be transferred from lecturer to student (hooks, 1994). The lecturer's physical presence is often anchored and immobile in the classroom, present only behind a desk or a lectern. The impact of this immobility is that lecturers are detached from students and inaccessible to them, further exacerbating the impression that knowledge is delivered by the lecturer to the waiting students.

The physical layout of the classroom and our position in it can be understood through de Certeau in the following way: the institution provides us with a classroom, and the lecturer and students are each meant to occupy a certain place within that: standing at the front of the room behind a lectern for the lecturer, seated at tables and chairs oriented to the front for the students. These classroom layouts and positions of actors may be the way the classroom space is produced, but it does not determine how it is consumed. Once we, lecturers and students alike, enter that room, it becomes ours for the duration of the timetabled session and this opens possibilities for us. Tables and chairs are not fixed to the floor, they can be moved and reorganised to suit the session needs. Granted, this takes time and coordination on the part of all involved, but doing so can yield interesting results that help to disrupt the expected behaviours associated with the TEF and its conceptualisation of teaching quality. Similarly, the immobility of the body of the lecturer and knowledge can be disrupted by the lecturer moving out from behind the lectern and engaging with students in the classroom. Moving our bodies out into the classroom brings with it the possibility of face-to-face communications and relationships (hooks, 1994) disrupting the perception of a largely transactional provider–consumer relationship as encouraged by the TEF and the wider UK higher education sector.

The layout of the classroom and our physical presence in it can help to establish a different basis of the lecturer–student interaction, moving away from the delivery of content and the supply of a product towards a space in which lecturers and students work together to discuss and create new knowledge. If this idea sounds familiar, it is because it has a long and rich history in educational thought and practice, developed through Paulo Freire's work (1993) and the subsequent explorations of many others working under the broad umbrella of critical pedagogy. Critical pedagogy does not aim to do away with the role of the lecturer in guiding the learning which occurs in the classroom, but to embrace the knowledge students already bring to the classroom. Examples of how to embrace students' knowledge are abound throughout literature on critical pedagogy and feminist and anarchist approaches to education. I would like to highlight Donnelly and Hogan's example of freehand drawing which I have adapted and used to great effect in several different university teaching contexts. Inspired by Freire's work, Donnelly and Hogan (2013) use freehand drawing at the beginning of their course on Irish politics to introduce all students to the wide variety of knowledges present in the classroom and to illustrate the ways in which each student contributes to a collective understanding of Irish politics. I have adapted the use of freehand drawing for an introductory session on the philosophy of education, asking the students to draw a response to the question: what is education? The advantages of the freehand drawing exercise are threefold: first, it shifts the focus away from me as a lecturer and disrupts the expectation that I will deliver an answer to the question and the students do not need to engage with it. Second, it places the students' knowledge as the foundation of the session. Third, it asks the students to take an active role in the session. Through the presentation of their knowledge in the drawings, students and I are able to start asking fundamental questions of one another about what we assume education to be and how it should operate. The drawing increases student involvement in the content of the session and takes seriously any contributions they make. While this meets calls for student satisfaction through the TEF, we do so in a way which the broader economic and neoliberal logic of the higher education sector cannot account for. The session is driven by a collaborative and dialogic approach to education rather than the neoliberal provider–consumer logic that permeates the TEF and thus is a form of resistance.

A further step along the path of student involvement in the creation of knowledge is for modules to be designed in collaboration between academics and students. What I present here is a confluence of different ideas including work on decolonising the curriculum (Students' Union, University College London, 2014), inspiration drawn from the Lincoln Social Science Centre in the United Kingdom (Neary & Winn, 2017; The Social Science Centre, Lincoln, n.d.) and various Occupy encampments (DiSalvo, 2013; Entin, et al., 2013; Mann, 2012). While a seemingly disparate collection of educational experiences, they share a commitment to radical democratic practice in education. Starting with the provocative video by students at University College London (UCL), UK, who challenge academia for its whiteness and racist curriculums that either ignore contributions to knowledge from non-white scholars, or include non-white scholars as a token gesture to diversity (Students' Union, University College London, 2014) and call on academia to decolonise the curriculum, which means reassessing and redesigning the curriculum from a starting point that does not assume the unquestionable status of a white canon. Doing so would mean taking into account the diversity of the students we work with and reflecting this in the content of courses, building a further connection through which students can recognise and contribute to the creation of alternative knowledges (Begum & Saini, 2019).

The move to decolonise curriculums is an important consideration in the design of modules and can be wedded to the radically democratic practices of Occupy and the Lincoln Social Science Centre. The teaching and learning occurring in Occupy encampments around the world and in Lincoln were reflections of the staff and students in their specific contexts and the teaching which took place was not at the behest of a single lecturer or teacher, but the result of collaborative democratic decision-making. At various Occupy encampments working groups were formed for the organisation and running of the camps, and in many cases, like that of Occupy Wall Street, this included a specific working group for educational projects (Blanchard, 2013; DiSalvo, 2013). The aim of these working groups was not to devise the educational programmes of the encampments, but to assist others who proposed courses. Operating through a nonhierarchical democratic approach, working groups would collaborate with participants from the encampments to support and promote the educational programmes suggested, with the educational moments of each encampment reflecting the context and make up of the encampment itself (Entin et al., 2013). The Social Science Centre (SSC) at Lincoln followed a similar nonhierarchical democratic approach to course design by establishing and operating as a cooperative. The aim of the SSC was to provide higher education level programmes with rigourous academic study, and to do this through collaborative programme design: 'All classes are participative and collaborative in order to ground enquiry in the experiences and knowledges of the participants. Student-scholars and teacher-scholars have opportunities to design courses together' (The Social Science Centre, Lincoln, n.d.). Areas of current knowledge were taken into account, but the educational content was not designed by someone in the role of a traditional lecturer prior to the establishment of the programmes. Much like the various

Occupy encampments, participants in the SSC worked together to design educational programmes and all were encouraged to contribute to the teaching and learning as part of the programme itself and the wider SSC (Neary & Winn, 2017).

Together, the push to decolonise the curriculum and the radically democratic approaches to education seen in Occupy and the SSC are a formidable tactic available to academics in resisting the TEF. These two elements of course design inspired one of my own modules, a first year course on philosophy of education. In this module I present a diverse long list of 14 different educational philosophers supported by a leaflet containing some key pieces of information about the thinker, their ideas and the session attached to them. In the first session of the module, it is the students who use this material to decide which nine thinkers they would like to study in more detail throughout the course. Within the confines of the UK higher education institution, there are various procedures I must follow in the validation of a module, including adherence to the broader Quality Assurance Agency guidelines for the degree programme, university guidelines on contact hours, module overview, learning outcomes, assessment design, etc., but by keeping the documentation on these deliberately vague I am able to leave enough space for student participation and collaborative module design. While it is not possible to take this collaboration to the same level as that found in Occupy or the SSC, I am able to offer students the chance to decide what they study. The impact of this is twofold: in the first instance, it creates space for students to access a wider variety and diversity of possible educational thinkers, helping decolonise the curriculum through the options of a variety of non-white and/or non-male philosophers. In the second instance, the collaborative and democratic approach offers students a greater agency and common ownership of the module, increasing the chance of positive results on the all-important TEF metrics of student satisfaction, while simultaneously undermining the broader social and political framework the TEF and higher education institutions operate in and through. Collaborative module design and ownership disrupts the underpinning logic permeating UK higher education institutions that it is the lecturer who designs and delivers courses and the students who receive knowledge and are educated in that process.

The tactics of classroom layout, physical position, freehand drawing and collaborative design explored above are presented as personal suggestions for resisting the TEF, rather than blueprints for action. In each case, the examples have enabled me to meet the institutionally imposed requirements of student satisfaction as reflected in mid- and end-of-term evaluations, while simultaneously consuming the classroom in a way that aligns with my understanding of the role of teaching and learning in higher education. The TEF as a strategy of English higher education institutions may appear pervasive but by embracing wiggery we are able to create alternative spaces and social practices to escape while remaining within. My contention here is that to practice wiggery, develop tactics and create fleeting spaces of resistance, we as academics often need to look for inspiration from beyond the immediate field of education. In the case of hooks and the lecturer's corporeal presence, this inspiration came through her engagement with feminist theories; for Donnelly and Hogan it was in embracing the possibilities of art, for the students at UCL it was post-colonial theory and for the Social Science Centre and Occupy it was forms of radically democratic politics. Perhaps this should not come as a surprise. Those of us working in the English higher education sector are immersed in a system which prioritises a very narrow conception of teaching and learning, and we need inspiration from beyond that immediate context. There is a second element that unites these different tactics and attempts to resist, and that is the recognition of our teaching and learning practice as something that is not and cannot be reduced to the metrics of the TEF. In the very action of looking beyond the borders of the place of the university and resisting the TEF as a strategy, we are *already* resisting the moves to constrain us. We are *already* operating in ways and means entirely unaccountable to and through the TEF as the dominant strategy of English higher education institutions through approaching our and others' teaching as something other than a means to the end of student satisfaction and a higher institutional TEF status.

REFERENCES

Amoore, L. (2013). *The politics of possibility. Risk and security beyond probability*. London: Duke University Press.

Ball, S. J. (2012). Performativity, commodification and commitment: An I-spy guide to the neoliberal university. *British Journal of Educational Studies*, 60(1), 17–28.

Begum, N., & Saini, R. (2019). Decolonising the curriculum. *Political Studies Review*, 17(2), 196–201.

Blanchard, D. (2013). Occupy education. *Radical Teacher*, 96(Spring), 59–63.

Brogan, A. J. (2017). The exilic classroom: Spaces of subversion. *Journal of Philosophy of Education*, 51(2), 510–523.

Buchanan, I. (2000). *Michel de Certeau. Cultural theorist*. London: SAGE Publications.

De Certeau, M. (1988). *The practice of everyday life*. London: University of California Press.

Department for Business, Innovation & Skills (2016). *Success as a knowledge Economy: Teaching excellence, social mobility and student choice*. London: Department for Business, Innovation & Skills.

DiSalvo, J. (2013). Political education - occupy Wall street's first year. *Radical Teacher*, *96*(Spring), 6–15.

Donnelly, P. F., & Hogan, J. (2013). Engaging students in the classroom: 'How can I know what I think until I see what I draw?' *European Political Science*, *12*, 365–383.

Entin, J., Ohmann, R., & O'Malley, S. (2013). Occupy and education: Introduction. *Radical Teacher*, *96*(Spring), 1–5.

Foucault, M. (1977). *Discipline and punish. The birth of the prison*. London: Penguin Books.

Freire, P. (1993). *Pedagogy of the oppressed*. London: Penguin Books.

French, A., & O'Leary, M. (Eds.). (2017). *Teaching excellence in higher education: Challenges, changes and the teaching excellence framework*. Bingley: Emerald Publishing Limited.

hooks, b. (1994). *Teaching to transgress: Education as the practice of freedom*. London: Routledge.

Heilbronn, R. (2013). Wigs, disguises and child's play: Solidarity recovered in education. *Ethics and Education*, *8*, 31–41.

Mann, L. (2012). On Occupy Wall Street. In A. Schrager Lang & D. Lang/Levitsky (Eds.), *Dreaming in public: Building the occupy movement* (pp. 108–111). Oxford: New Internationalist Publications.

Neary, M., & Winn, J. (2017). There is an alternative. A report on an action research project to develop a framework for co-operative hgiher education. *Learning and Teaching*, *10*(1), 87–105.

Student's Union, University College London. (2014). *Why is my curriculum white?* London: University College London.

The Social Science Centre, Lincoln. (n.d). About us. Retrieved from https://socialsciencecentre.wordpress.com/about/. Accessed on August 2019.

Universities UK. (2015). *Patterns and trends in higher education 2015*. London: Universities UK.

POSTSCRIPT

Amanda French and Kate Carruthers Thomas

The essays in this collection have offered alternative ways of thinking about teaching and learning in higher education (HE) that put centre stage the challenges of a diverse sector. In the light of that diversity, the collection has sought to expand on current institutional responses to the TEF, which have primarily coalesced around initiatives and activities that directly, and largely uncritically, contribute to the collection of metrics-based data and additional contextual information required for TEF submissions (Cui, French, & O'Leary, 2019; Vivian et al., 2019). Whilst these reports confirm that the TEF has undoubtedly begun to change institutional practices, it is clear that the changes it has wrought work, in the main, to reflect TEF priorities. As stated in the Preface, for those with TEF Gold, and to a lesser extent TEF Silver, TEF rankings help to 'polish' each institution's image for marketing and recruitment purposes, whilst inevitably tarnishing those who are awarded TEF Bronze. This focus on the commercial effect of the TEF is, however, in stark contrast to Sir Michael Barber's early assertion that the TEF should:

> *...be a catalyst for improvement of, and innovation*
> *in, the quality of teaching ... [to] generate informed*
> *dialogue about teaching quality both within*
> *institutions and between them. (2017).*

Recording, exploring and valuing the many different experiences of teaching and learning that undoubtedly exist in HE would clearly be a valuable way of opening up a dialogue about 'teaching excellence' in all its various guises. Sharing innovative and effective practice across institutions would undoubtedly help act as a catalyst for change and improvement across universities, without reducing the concept of 'good practice' in teaching to a 'one-size-fits-all' formula. However, there is currently very little evidence of Barber's anticipated dialogue or innovation around teaching, excellent or otherwise, arising out the TEF. Indeed, recent changes to TEF processes have tended to shift attention away from even a cursory debate about 'teaching excellence' towards a greater emphasis on measuring and comparing student outcomes and post-degree salaries, without ever attempting to articulate what the relationship between them. As O'Leary and French (2017) point out in the final section of their report into staff perceptions and experiences of the TEF:

> *For an alternative model of teaching excellence to*
> *make a meaningful and authentic contribution to*
> *stimulating and supporting the sustained*
> *improvement of teaching quality, it would require*
> *academic staff and students to work together to*
> *develop a shared understanding of what matters to*
> *teaching and learning.*

The essays in this collection have hopefully begun to make one such 'meaningful and authentic contribution to stimulating and supporting the sustained improvement of teaching quality' (O'Leary & French, 2017). The gaze of our authors has rested on the hard work and nuanced expertise that goes into creating teaching in diverse HE contexts, across a range of disciplines, to vastly different kinds of students by different kinds of staff. Rather than judging and measuring that teaching, the emphasis here has been on asking questions and exploring ways of thinking about teaching in HE in more complex and inclusive ways.

However, this collection also acts to remind us of Kate Carruthers Thomas's warning in the Preface that 'We must also appreciate what is obscured', by the kind of institutional polishing that the TEF encourages. To this end we have drawn attention to how TEF underplays the significance of both institutional differences and their differing, but completely legitimates priorities and specialisms. Critiquing notions of 'deliverology' and 'performativity' have helped crystallise how TEF focuses on delivering a set of government priorities which measure only what it values and value only what it measures. We have tried to draw attention to the fact that while the TEF may value student outcomes (a laudable aim), it does so primarily in terms of measuring what graduates earn. In doing so, it ignores not only marked salary variations between different occupations but also other significant factors that affect students' potential earning power, such as their own social and economic backgrounds and the reputational prestige conferred by attendance at some HE institutions. The TEF may seek to represent what students think about their university experiences, especially around the teaching they have received; however, it homogenises those experiences through the blunt instrumentalism of the NSS. It seeks to identify excellent teaching but fails to recognise the different contextual and personal factors that inform how teaching staff are perceived and the very diverse (and often perverse) conditions under which they carry out their teaching.

Focussing attention on what sits behind the reflected glare of the TEF involves acknowledging the deficiencies and deficits in the TEF's current means of assessment and evaluation. In the Preface, Kate Carruthers Thomas drew attention to Barad's (2007) observation that 'the optic/apparatus for observations will determine what is seen' as a way of understanding why the TEF is inherently discriminatory and limited as an evaluative tool. However, Barad also advocates using the idea of 'diffraction' which she defines as a commitment to observing 'patterns of difference' (Barad, 2007, p. 29) in what is measured and the effects of the differences on the process of measuring. To this end then, the notion of 'diversity deficits' in this collection is diffractive, in that the essays all pay attention to difference. Not only that, they insist on a fuller appreciation than the TEF could ever offer, of what diversity in HE's reach, student body and workforce can teach us all about fair and accessible teaching and learning practices and institutional processes and the part they can play in creating and sharing effective, even excellent teaching.

REFERENCES

Barad, K. (2007). *Meeting the universe halfway: Quantum physics and the entanglement of matter and meaning*. Durham: Duke University Press.

O'Leary, M., & French, A. (Eds.). (2017). *Excellence in higher education, challenges, changes and the teaching excellence framework*. Bingley: Emerald Publishing Limited.

Cui, V., French, A., & O'Leary, M. (2019). A missed opportunity? How the UK's teaching excellence framework fails to capture the voice of university staff. *Studies in Higher Education*, doi:10.1080/03075079.2019.1704721. Retrieved from https://srhe.tandfonline.com/doi/abs/10.1080/03075079.2019.1704721?journalCode=cshe20#. Xu91R2hKja. Accessed online January, 2020.

Vivian, D., James, A. S., Salamons, D., Hazel, Z., Felton, J., & Whittaker, S. (2019). *Evaluation of Provider-level TEF 2016-17 (Year 2): Measuring the initial impact of the TEF on the Higher Education landscape research report. Department for Education.*

ABOUT THE CONTRIBUTORS

Dr. Brendan Bartram is Reader in Education at the University of Wolverhampton. His research and publications cover a wide range of issues which reflect the eclectic nature of Education Studies. Focussing primarily on comparative issues in Higher Education (HE), Brendan's research has explored university student mobility, support and motivation.

Dr. Andrew Brogan has a background in political theory and his research interests are rooted in critical pedagogy, anarchism and subversive classroom practices. Alongside and through his teaching, he continues to explore radical pedagogical approaches in HE as he works to bring theory and practice together to help inform personal and social change.

Dr. Kate Carruthers Thomas has worked in UK HE since 1990; in continuing education and widening participation until 2011, thereafter as an academic in the social sciences. She is currently Senior Research Fellow in Social Sciences at Birmingham City University, specialising in interdisciplinary enquiry into contemporary HE, inequalities and gender. Kate has presented her work widely in national and international fora and uses poetry and graphics as well as conventional methods to disseminate her research. Kate is also the lead for the Athena SWAN gender equality agenda at Birmingham City University.

Julian Crockford: Until recently, Julian managed the Widening Participation Research and Evaluation Unit at the University of Sheffield. He is now Chief Programmes Officer at Villiers Park Educational Trust. He is also halfway through writing up a professional doctorate on the evaluation of widening participation and inclusive learning and teaching activities.

Dr. Amanda French has worked in higher, further, adult education and the voluntary sector in the West Midlands for 30 years. She has worked in partnerships and taught across a wide range of settings and agencies including schools, community centres, voluntary and community groups, as well as colleges and universities. Amanda is currently Head of Professional Development, Research and Enterprise at Birmingham City University's School of Education and Social Work and is a Reader in Teaching and Learning. Her personal research interests include academic writing practices and development, HE policy, social justice in education and creative critical pedagogy and methodologies. She has published and presented on her work nationally and internationally.

Leanne Hunt studied Psychology at the University of Bradford, participated in the Peer Assisted Learning Scheme as a student and now works at the institution in Peer Support. First in the family to attend university and is currently studying a Masters in Careers Guidance at the University of Huddersfield.

Dr. Jenny Lawrence, M.Ed, PFHEA, AFSEDA studied Philosophy and Gender Studies at the University of Hull, her local university. The first in her family to go to university, she has devoted her academic career to making the academy accessible to staff and students from backgrounds underrepresented in HE.

Joanne Moore has undertaken a range of research and evaluation to support the take-up of learning and skills, retention and achievement. She is a Research Fellow at the Centre for Social Mobility, University of Exeter, and her most recent work has supported equity of access and success in HE.

Anna Mountford-Zimdars is a Professor in Education, Principal Fellow HEA, and has served as widening participation expert on two rounds of the national Teaching Excellence Panel and Director of the Centre for Social Mobility at the University of Exeter. She has published widely and contributes to policy debates.

Dr. John Sanders, Director of ARC Network (2011–2020), was Assistant Director of Aimhigher Greater Manchester (2006–2011) and a leading figure in the 'Open College Network' movement (1981–2006). He has also worked as an OU Associate Lecturer (1985–2019) and was a member of the QAA's Access Recognition and Licensing Committee (2012–2018).

Hollie Shaw studied Biochemistry and Human Biology at University Centre Scunthorpe and Sheffield Hallam University. She is currently completing a PhD in Microbiology at the University of Sheffield. She was the first in her family to attend university as a mature student.

Donovan Synmoie, SFHEA, started his academic career in Film Studies before progressing to Educational Development. He has worked to raise awareness of the Black Asian and Minority Ethnic staff and student university experience and widen BAME participation in university work and study. His work is currently focussed on closing the awarding gap at the University of Greenwich.

INDEX